CGP has the summer term sorted!

Reception Maths doesn't need to be boring — here at CGP we like to look on the sunny side of things... and that's where this marvellous book comes in.

We've packed it with Maths activities — one for every day of the summer term. Better yet, each covers a skill from the Early Years curriculum.

Plus, we've included examples and bright, colourful pictures so pupils are sure to stay engaged. It's ideal for in-class practice, homework... and more!

What CGP is all about

Our sole aim here at CGP is to produce the highest quality books — carefully written, immaculately presented and dangerously close to being funny.

Then we work our socks off to get them out to you — at the cheapest possible prices.

Contents

☑ Use the tick boxes to help keep a record of which tests have been attempted.

Week 1
☑ Day 1 1
☑ Day 2 2
☑ Day 3 3
☑ Day 4 4
☑ Day 5 5

Week 2
☑ Day 1 6
☑ Day 2 7
☑ Day 3 8
☑ Day 4 9
☑ Day 5 10

Week 3
☑ Day 1 11
☑ Day 2 12
☑ Day 3 13
☑ Day 4 14
☑ Day 5 15

Week 4
☑ Day 1 16
☑ Day 2 17
☑ Day 3 18
☑ Day 4 19
☑ Day 5 20

Week 5
☑ Day 1 21
☑ Day 2 22
☑ Day 3 23
☑ Day 4 24
☑ Day 5 25

Week 6
☑ Day 1 26
☑ Day 2 27
☑ Day 3 28
☑ Day 4 29
☑ Day 5 30

Week 7
☑ Day 1 31
☑ Day 2 32
☑ Day 3 33
☑ Day 4 34
☑ Day 5 35

Week 8
☑ Day 1 36
☑ Day 2 37
☑ Day 3 38
☑ Day 4 39
☑ Day 5 40

Week 9

- [✓] Day 1 41
- [✓] Day 2 42
- [✓] Day 3 43
- [✓] Day 4 44
- [✓] Day 5 45

Week 10

- [✓] Day 1 46
- [✓] Day 2 47
- [✓] Day 3 48
- [✓] Day 4 49
- [✓] Day 5 50

Week 11

- [✓] Day 1 51
- [✓] Day 2 52
- [✓] Day 3 53
- [✓] Day 4 54
- [✓] Day 5 55

Week 12

- [✓] Day 1 56
- [✓] Day 2 57
- [✓] Day 3 58
- [✓] Day 4 59
- [✓] Day 5 60

Answers 61

Published by CGP

ISBN: 978 1 78908 760 4

Editors: Martha Bozic, Michael Bushell, Liam Dyer
Reviewers: Sharon Gulliver and Emma Wright

With thanks to Glenn Rogers for the proofreading.

With thanks to Lottie Edwards for the copyright research.

Cover and Graphics used throughout the book © www.edu-clips.com
Clipart from Corel®

Printed by Elanders Ltd, Newcastle upon Tyne.
Based on the classic CGP style created by Richard Parsons.

Text, design, layout and original illustrations © Coordination Group Publications Ltd. (CGP) 2021
All rights reserved.

Photocopying this book is not permitted, even if you have a CLA licence.
Extra copies are available from CGP with next day delivery • 0800 1712 712 • www.cgpbooks.co.uk

How to Use this Book

- This book contains 60 daily practice tests.

- We've split them into 12 sections — that's roughly one for each week of the Reception Summer term.

- Each week is made up of 5 tests, so there's one for every school day of the term (Monday – Friday).

- Each test should take about 10 minutes to complete.

- The tests contain a mix of topics from Reception Maths. New topics are gradually introduced as you go through the book.

- The tests increase in difficulty as you go through the book.

- Each test looks something like this:

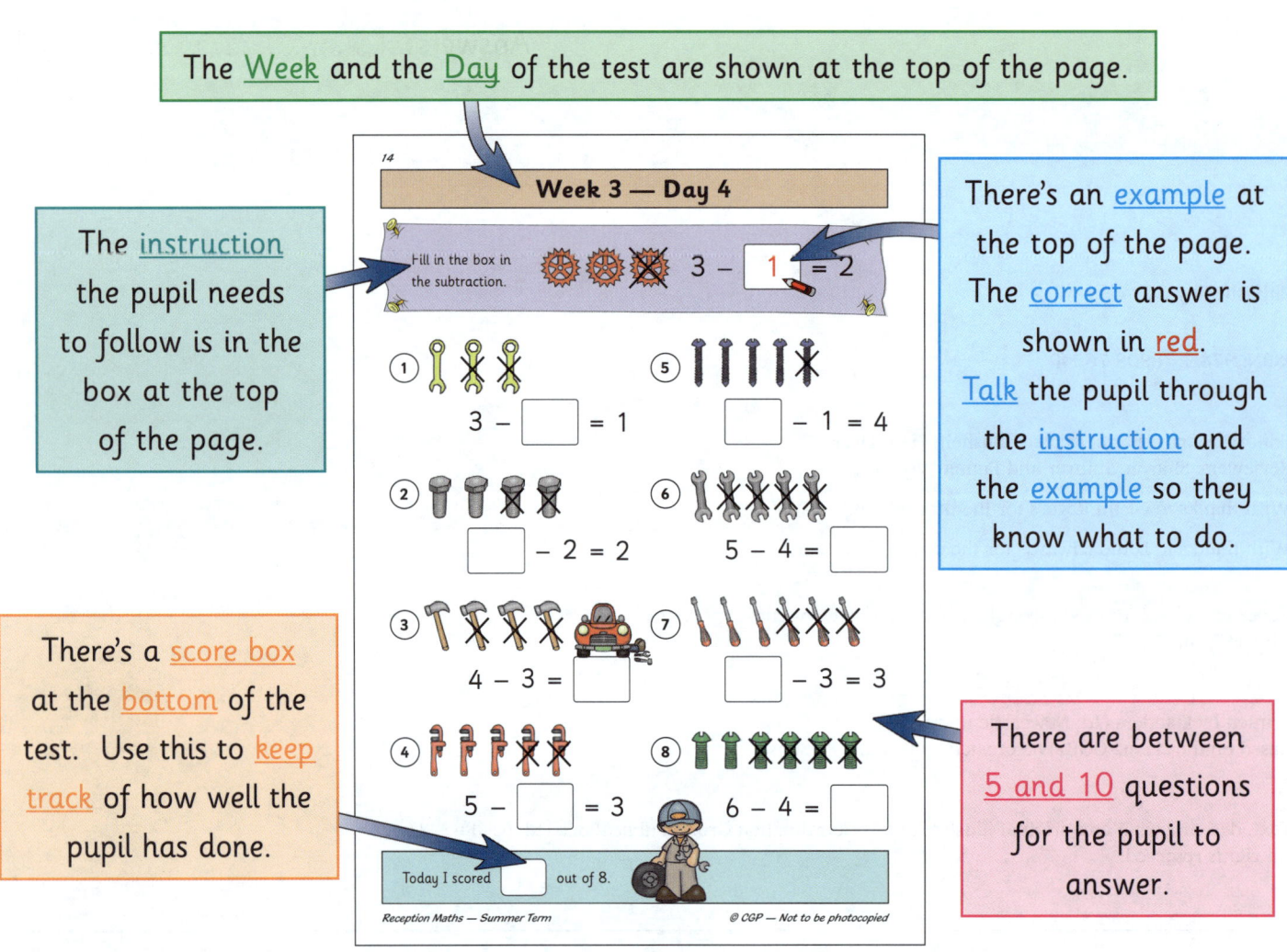

The Week and the Day of the test are shown at the top of the page.

The instruction the pupil needs to follow is in the box at the top of the page.

There's an example at the top of the page. The correct answer is shown in red. Talk the pupil through the instruction and the example so they know what to do.

There's a score box at the bottom of the test. Use this to keep track of how well the pupil has done.

There are between 5 and 10 questions for the pupil to answer.

Week 1 — Day 1

Draw lines to join the numbers you say.   Count from 3 to 6.

① Count from 2 to 5.

2	3	6
1	4	5

④ Count from 6 to 3.

6	5	3
7	4	2

② Count from 5 to 8.

4	6	9
5	7	8

⑤ Count from 11 to 7.

10	8	6
11	9	7

③ Count from 10 to 14.

10	13	15
11	12	14

⑥ Count from 13 to 9.

13	12	9
14	11	10

Today I scored ☐ out of 6.

Week 1 — Day 2

Double the number of spots on the butterfly.

1

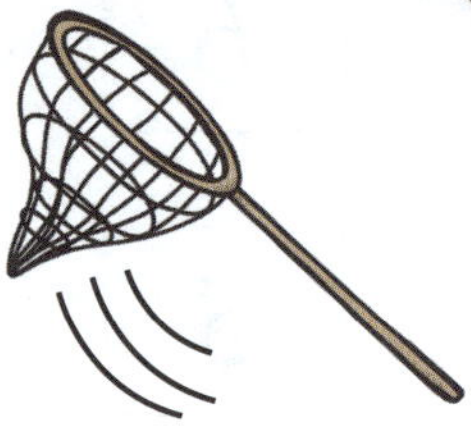

2

3

4

5

6

Today I scored [ ] out of 6.

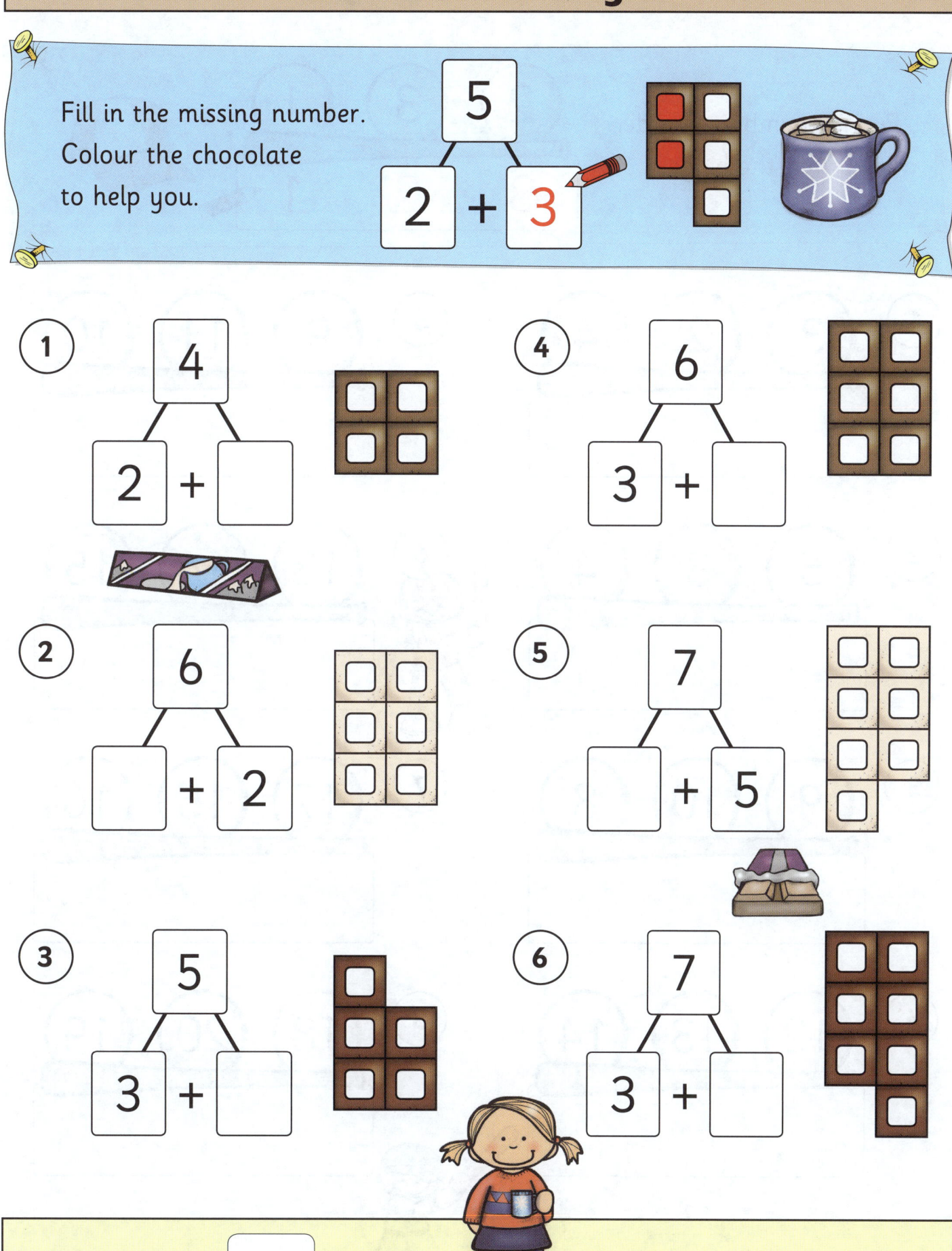

Week 1 — Day 4

Put the numbers in order. Start with the biggest.

2 3 1 → 3 2 1

1) 3 2 4 →

2) 5 3 4 →

3) 9 10 8 →

4) 12 13 14 →

5) 9 11 10 →

6) 13 14 15 →

7) 17 15 16 →

8) 18 20 19 →

Today I scored ☐ out of 8.

Week 1 — Day 5

Add together the numbers. Use the stars to help you.

★★★★ ★★
4 + 2 = 6

1) ★ ★★
   1 + 2 = ☐

2) ★★ ★
   2 + 1 = ☐

3) ★ ★★★
   1 + 3 = ☐

4) ★★★ ★★
   3 + 2 = ☐

5) ★★★★ ★
   4 + 1 = ☐

6) ★★
   0 + 2 = ☐

7) ★★ ★★★
   2 + 3 = ☐

8) ★ ★★★★
   1 + 4 = ☐

9) ★★★★★
   5 + 0 = ☐

10) ★★★ ★★★
    3 + 3 = ☐

Today I scored ☐ out of 10.

Week 2 — Day 1

Circle the cars in the right positions.

1st and 2nd

① 1st and 3rd

② 3rd and 4th

③ 2nd and 5th

④ 1st and 4th

⑤ 3rd and 5th

⑥ 4th and 6th

Today I scored ☐ out of 6.

Reception Maths — Summer Term

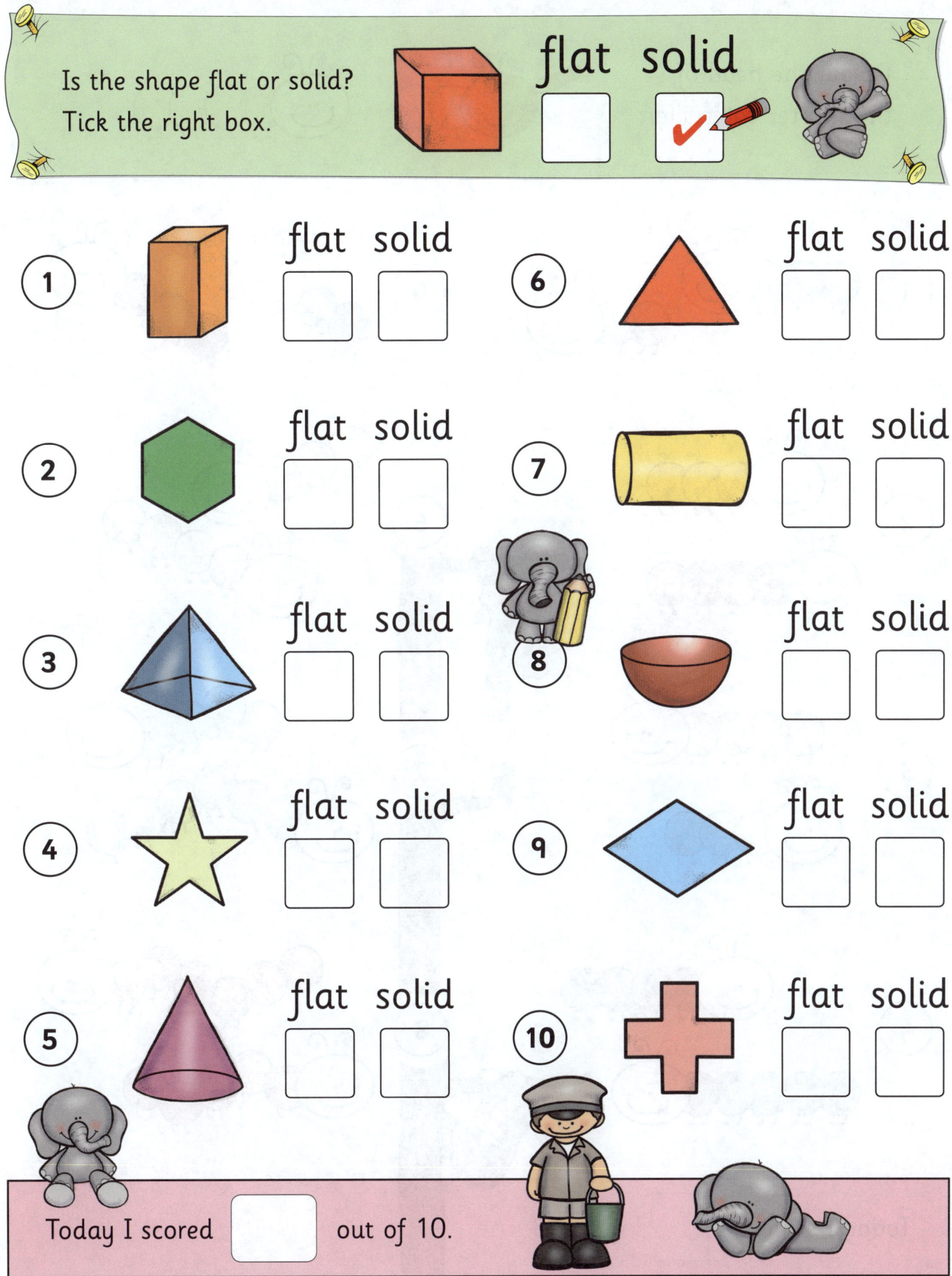

Week 2 — Day 3

Colour the head of the shorter caterpillar.

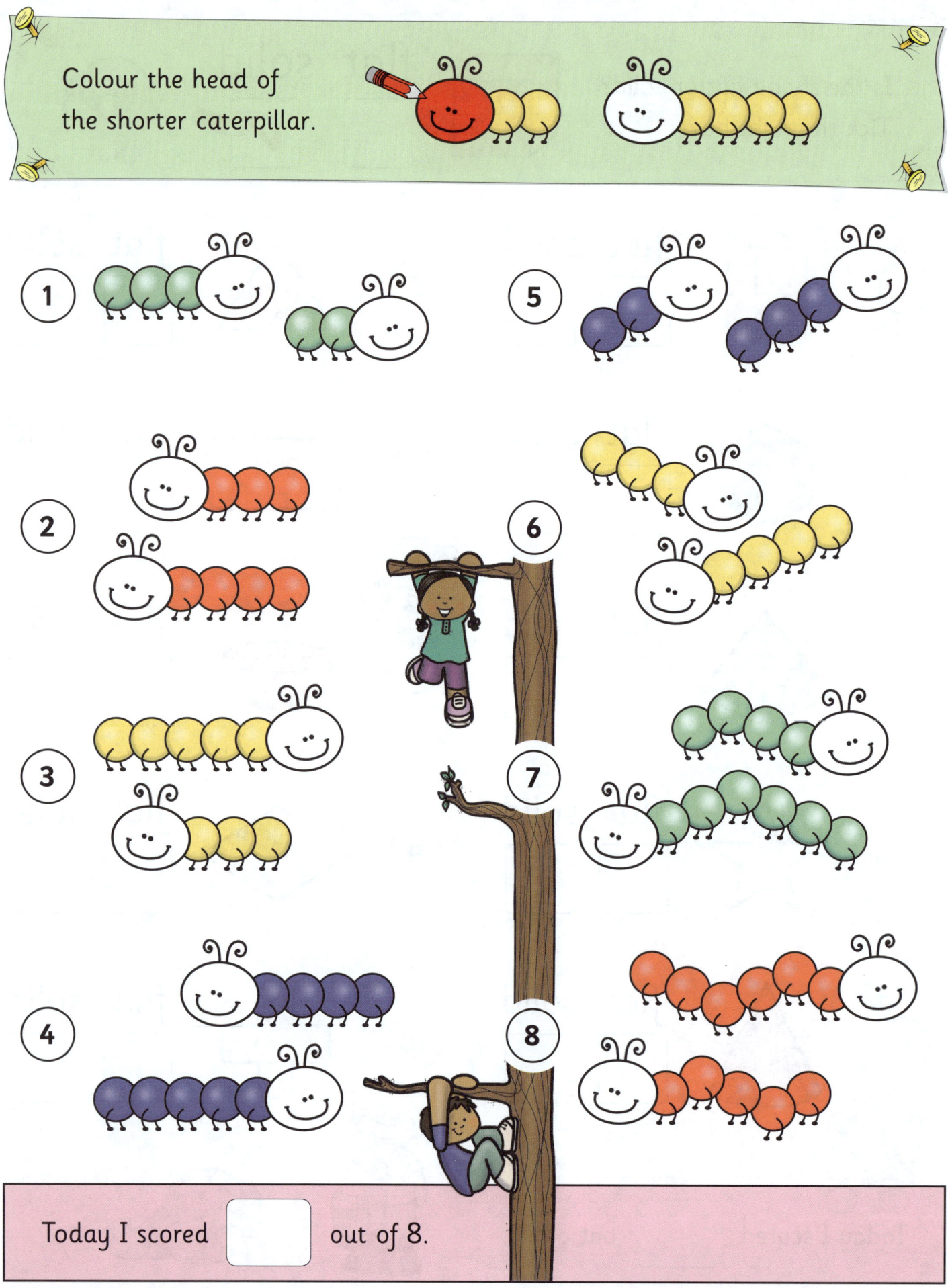

Today I scored ☐ out of 8.

Week 2 — Day 4

Cross out half of the pies.

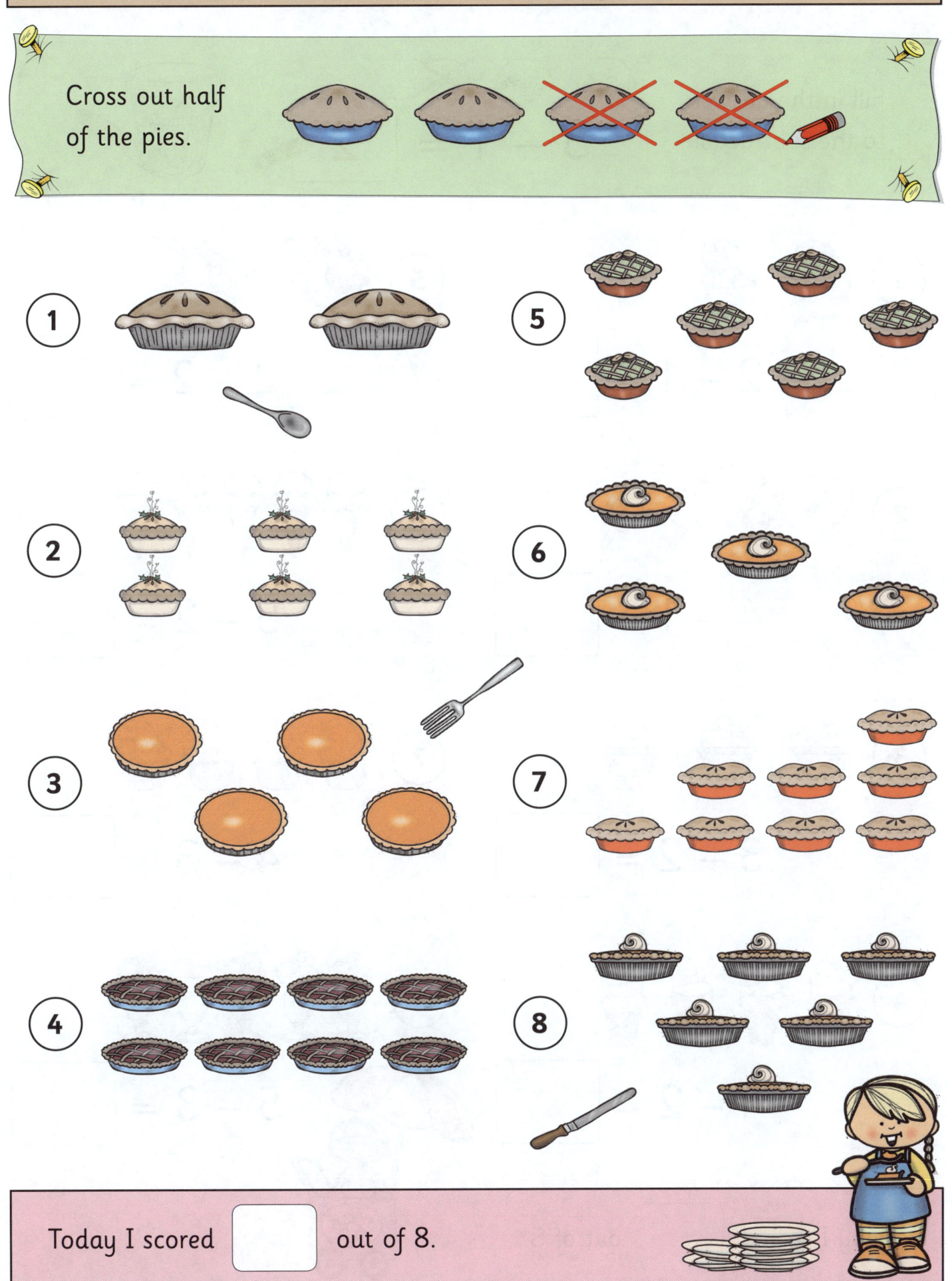

Today I scored ☐ out of 8.

Week 2 — Day 5

Fill in the answer to the subtraction.

     3 − 1 = 2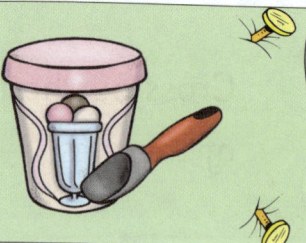

1)

2 − 1 = ☐

5)

2 − 2 = ☐

2)

4 − 1 = ☐

6)

5 − 2 = ☐

3)

3 − 2 = ☐

7)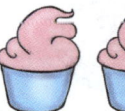

4 − 3 = ☐

4)

4 − 2 = ☐

8)

5 − 3 = ☐

Today I scored ☐ out of 8.

Reception Maths — Summer Term © CGP — Not to be photocopied

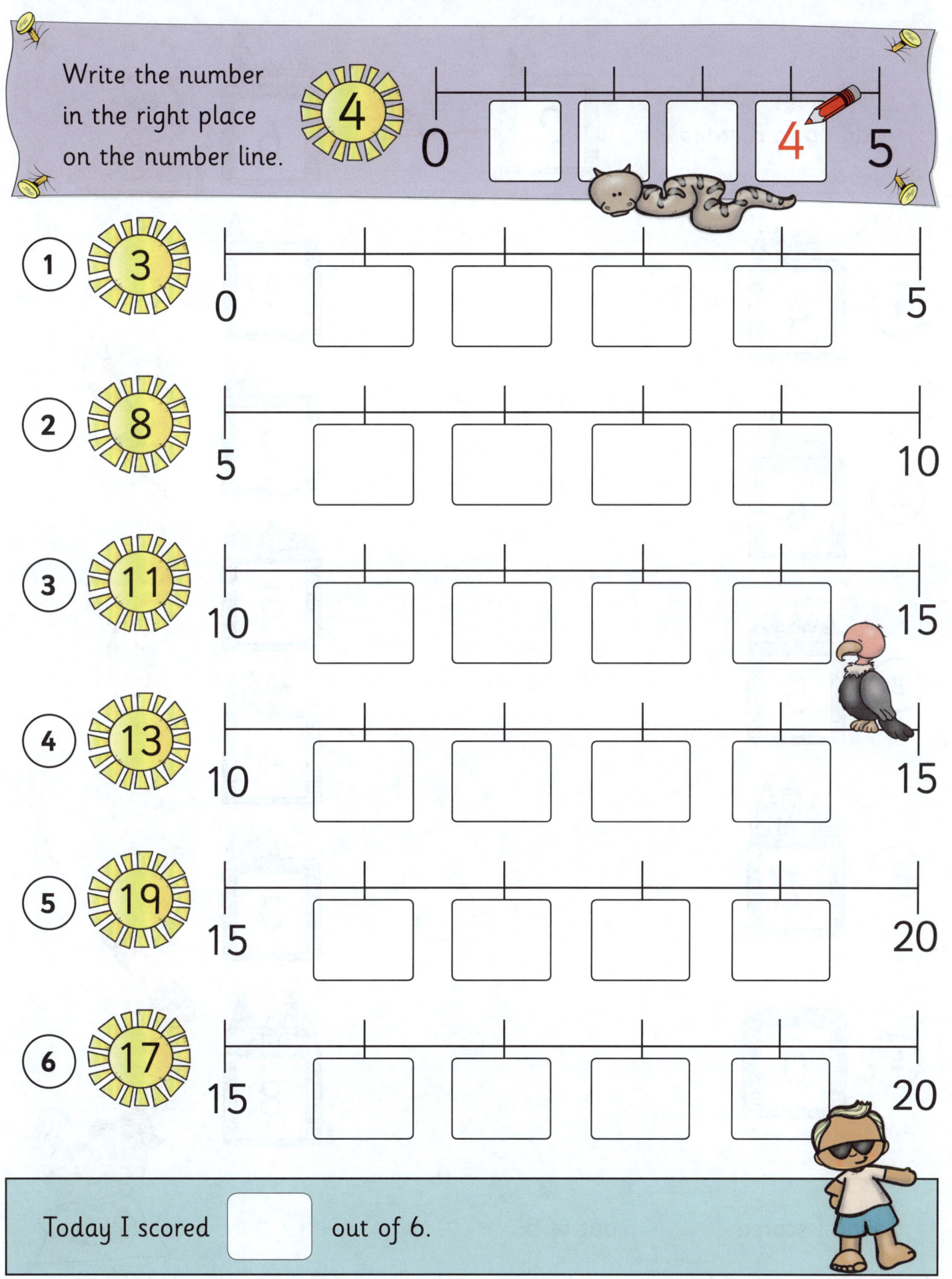

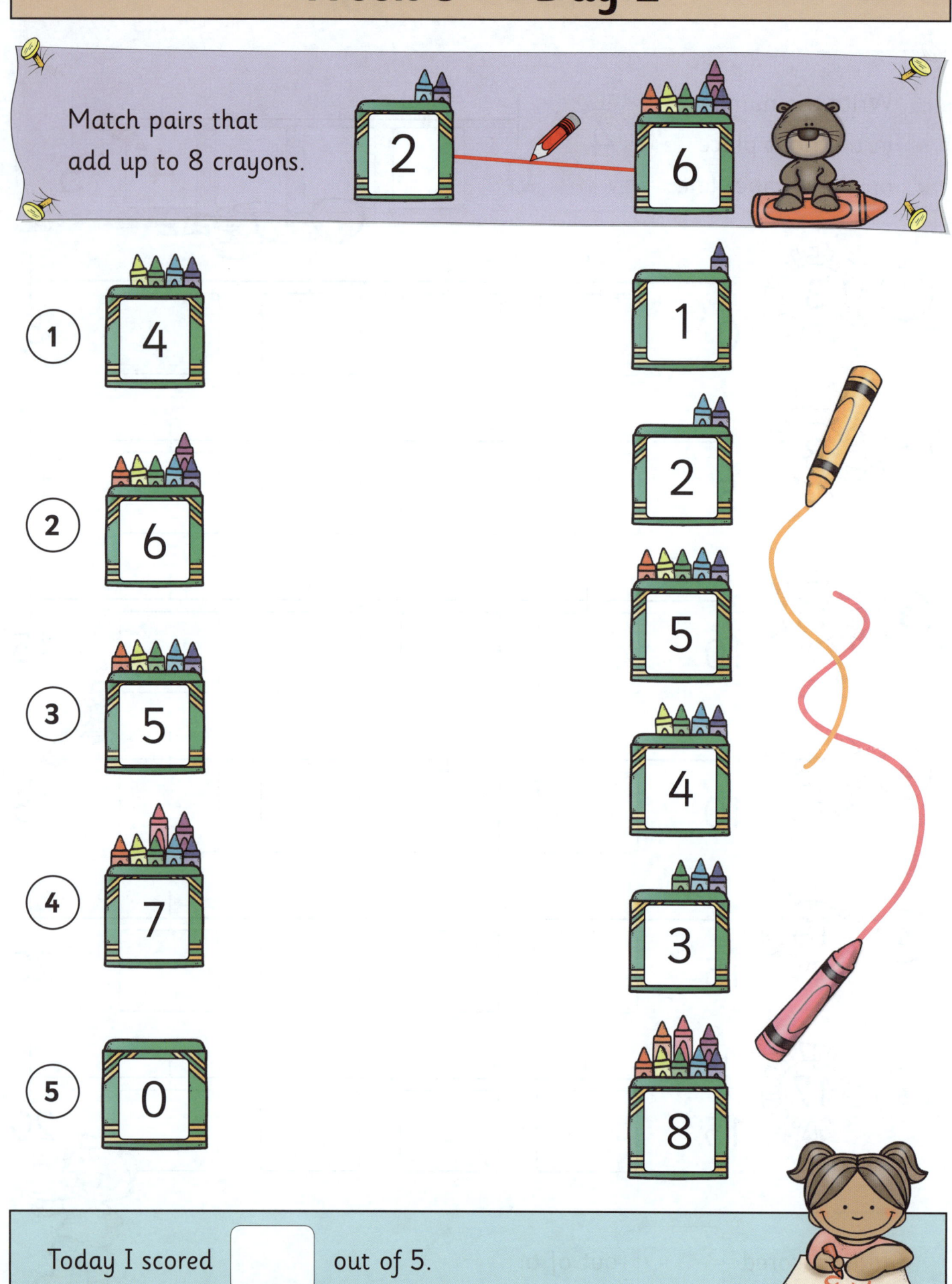

Week 3 — Day 3

Circle the object heavier than the one in the box. mug stamp **bath** (circled)

1.   cat    worm    ship   

2.  pear    truck     button

3.   drum    coin    castle    pin

4.  shoe    leaf 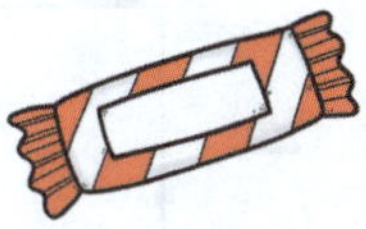    sweet    lion

5.  phone    card    acorn   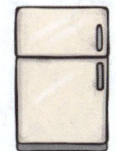 fridge

Today I scored ☐ out of 5.

© CGP — Not to be photocopied   Reception Maths — Summer Term

Week 3 — Day 4

Fill in the box in the subtraction.  3 − 1 = 2

1)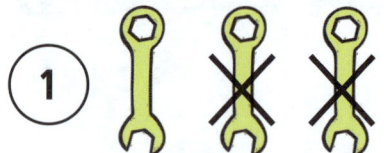
3 − ☐ = 1

2)
☐ − 2 = 2

3)
4 − 3 = ☐

4)
5 − ☐ = 3

5)
☐ − 1 = 4

6)
5 − 4 = ☐

7)
☐ − 3 = 3

8)
6 − 4 = ☐

Today I scored ☐ out of 8.

Reception Maths — Summer Term

Week 3 — Day 5

Draw more red cups to make two equal groups.

1

5

2

6

3

7

4

8

Today I scored  out of 8.

Week 4 — Day 1

Add the numbers together. Use the discs to help you.

1 + 2 = 3

1) 3 + 1 =

2) 4 + 2 =

3) 2 + 0 =

4) 5 + 1 =

5) 4 + 3 =

6) 6 + 1 =

7) 0 + 4 =

8) 2 + 4 =

9) 5 + 3 =

10) 4 + 4 =

Today I scored ☐ out of 10.

Week 4 — Day 2

Fill in the box. Use the pictures to help you. Double 1 is [2]

1) Double 3 is [ ]

2) Double 2 is [ ]

3) Double 5 is [ ]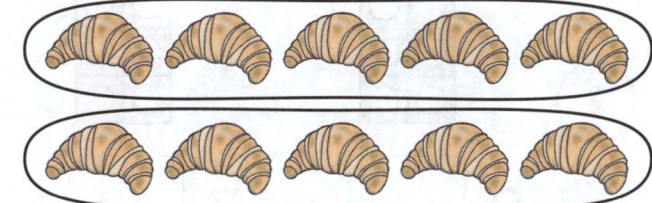

4) Double 4 is [ ]

5) Double 6 is [ ]

Today I scored [ ] out of 5.

Week 4 — Day 3

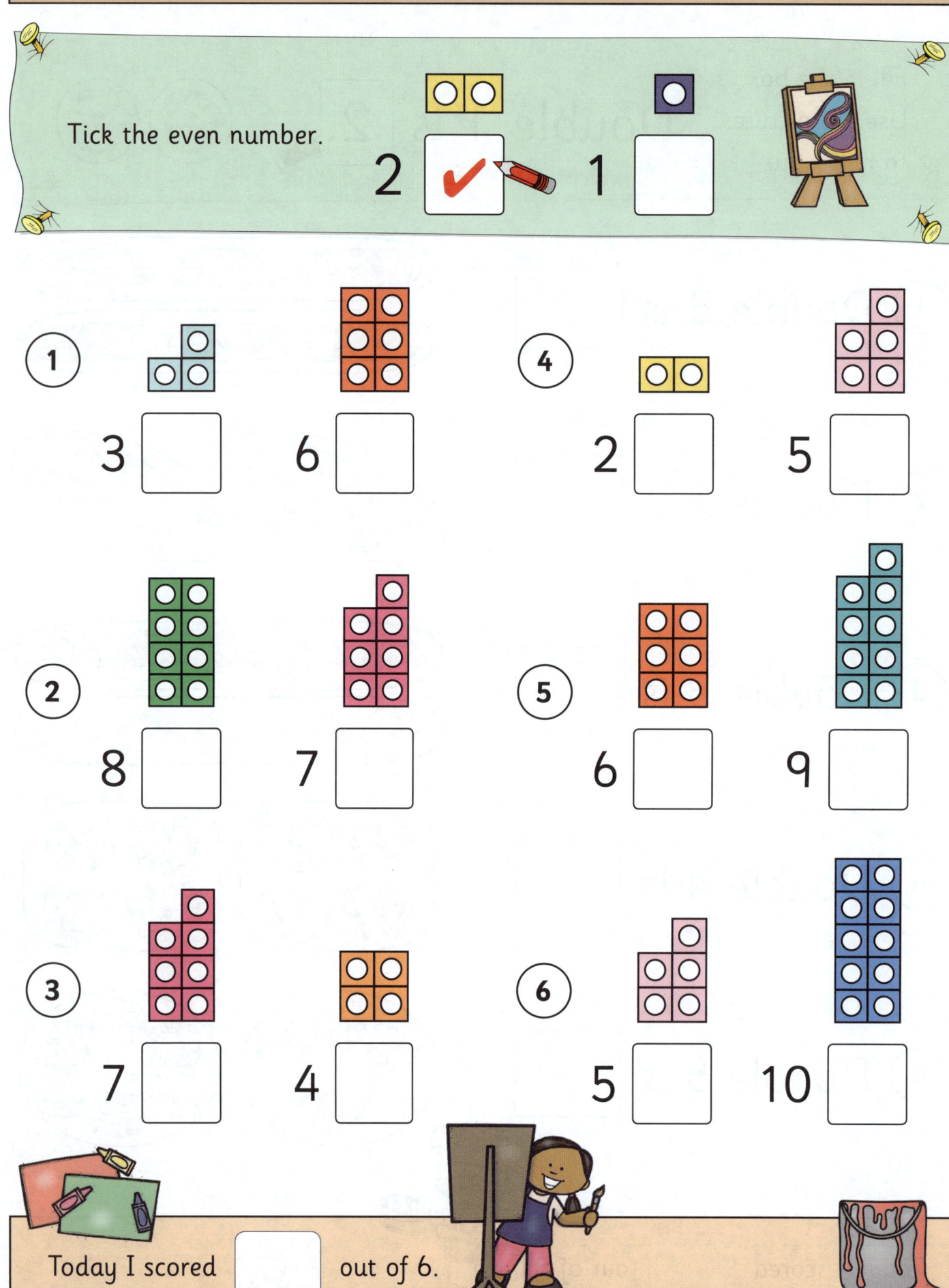

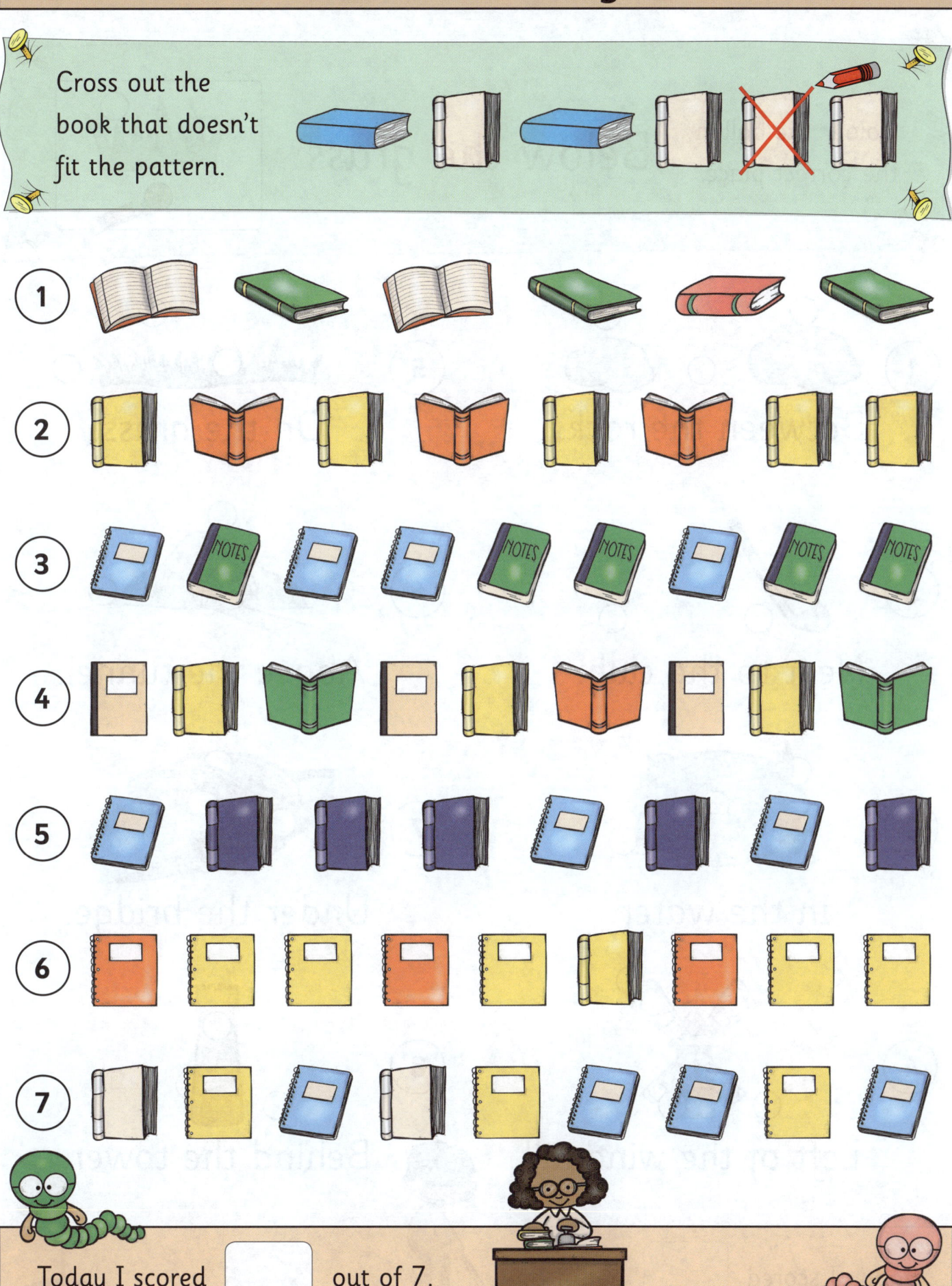

Week 4 — Day 5

Colour the ball in the correct place. **Below the grass.**

1. 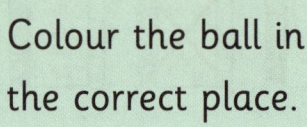 Between the rocks.

2.  Next to the club.

3.  In the water.

4.  Left of the windmill.

5.  On the grass.

6.  Above the tunnel.

7.  Under the bridge.

8.  Behind the tower.

Today I scored ☐ out of 8.

Week 5 — Day 1

Fill in the box to make a sum that adds to 9.

6 + 3

1) 8 + ☐

2) 7 + ☐

3) 5 + ☐

4) 3 + ☐

5) 4 + ☐

6) 9 + ☐

7) 1 + ☐

8) 2 + ☐

Today I scored ☐ out of 8.

Week 5 — Day 2

Match the object to the correct word.

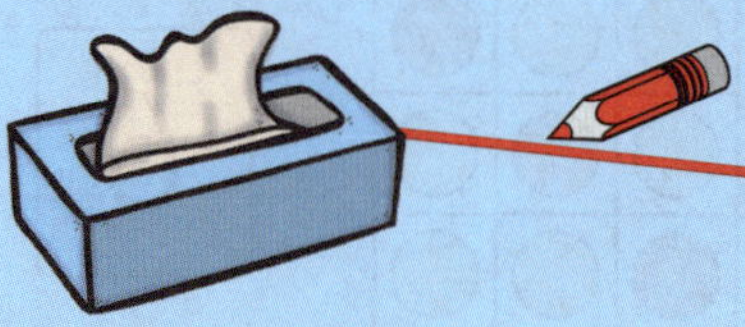

1. (battery) — cylinder
2. (ball) — sphere
3. (pyramid) — pyramid
4. (box) — cube
5. (cone) — cone

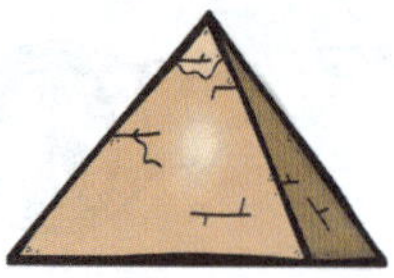

Words:
- cuboid
- cylinder
- square
- cone
- sphere
- cube
- triangle
- pyramid

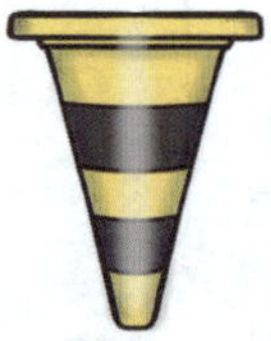

Today I scored ☐ out of 5.

Reception Maths — Summer Term

Week 5 — Day 3

Fill in the box. Use the pictures to help you.

Half of 2 is 1

① Half of 4 is ☐

② Half of 6 is ☐

③ Half of 8 is ☐

④ Half of 10 is ☐

⑤ Half of 12 is ☐

Today I scored ☐ out of 5.

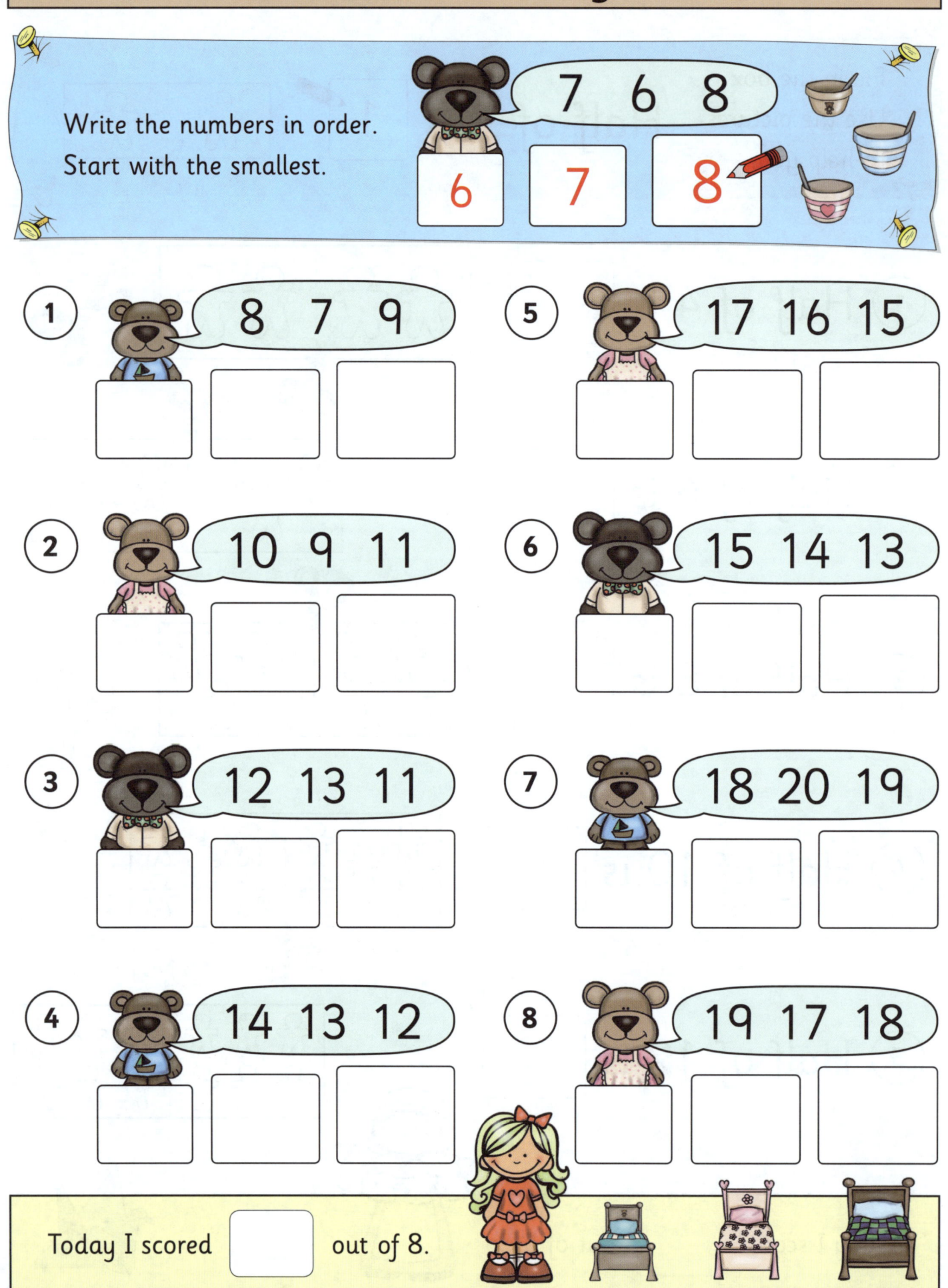

Week 5 — Day 5

Write the answer to the subtraction.

1.
2.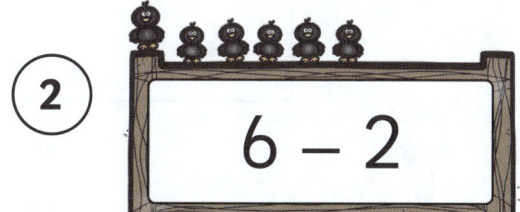
3.
4.
5.

6.
7.
8.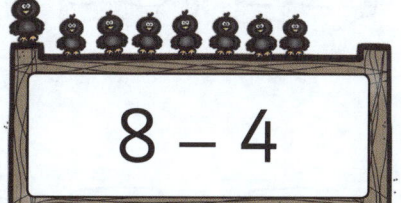
9.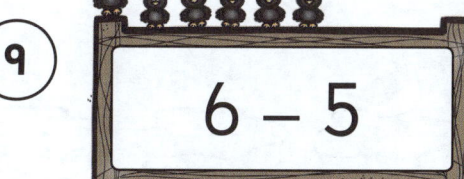
10.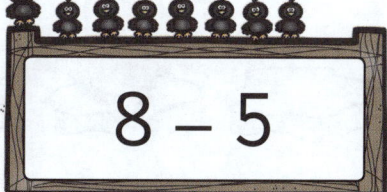

Today I scored ☐ out of 10.

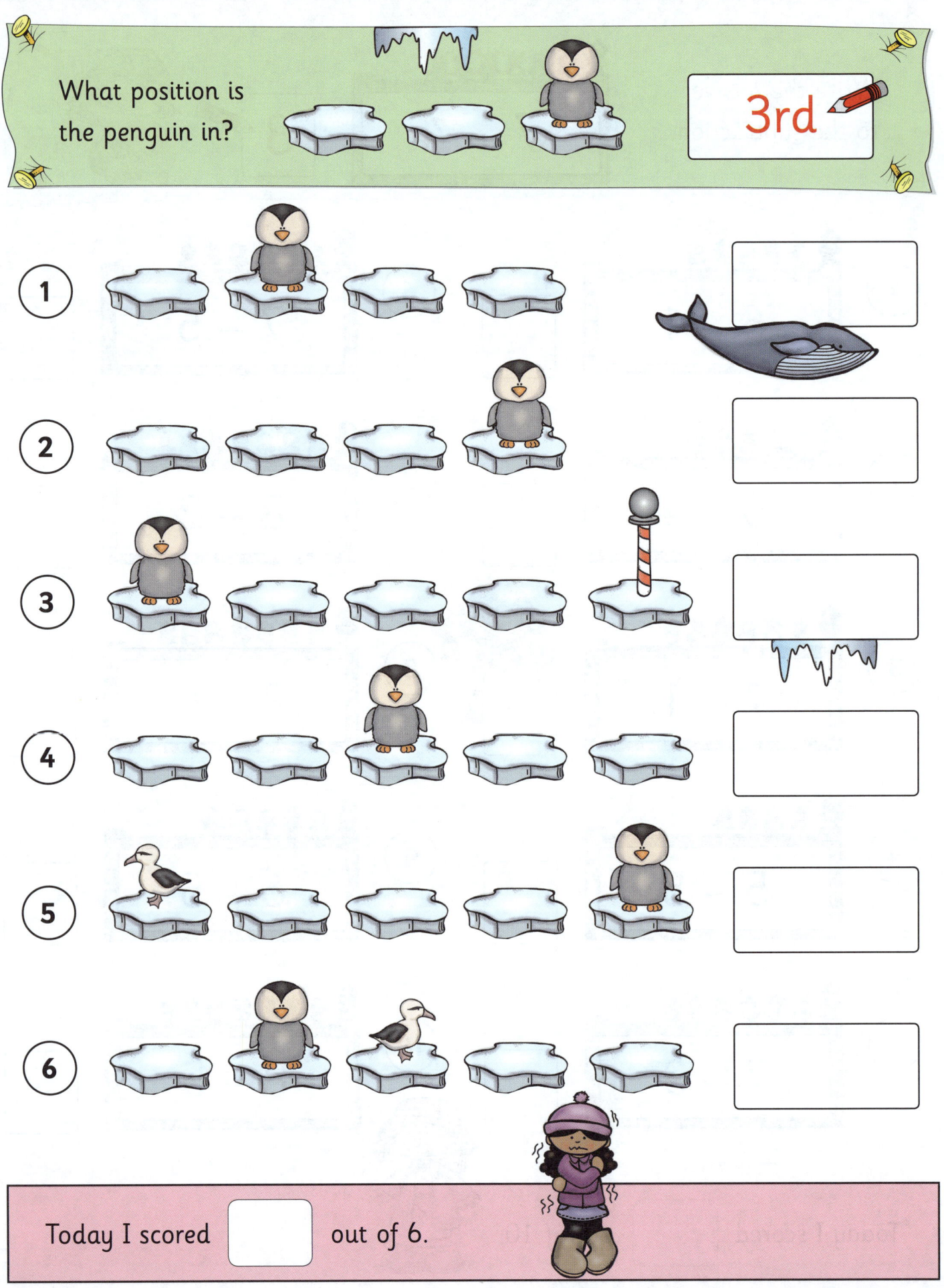

Week 6 — Day 2

Draw an arrow to show the number on the number line.

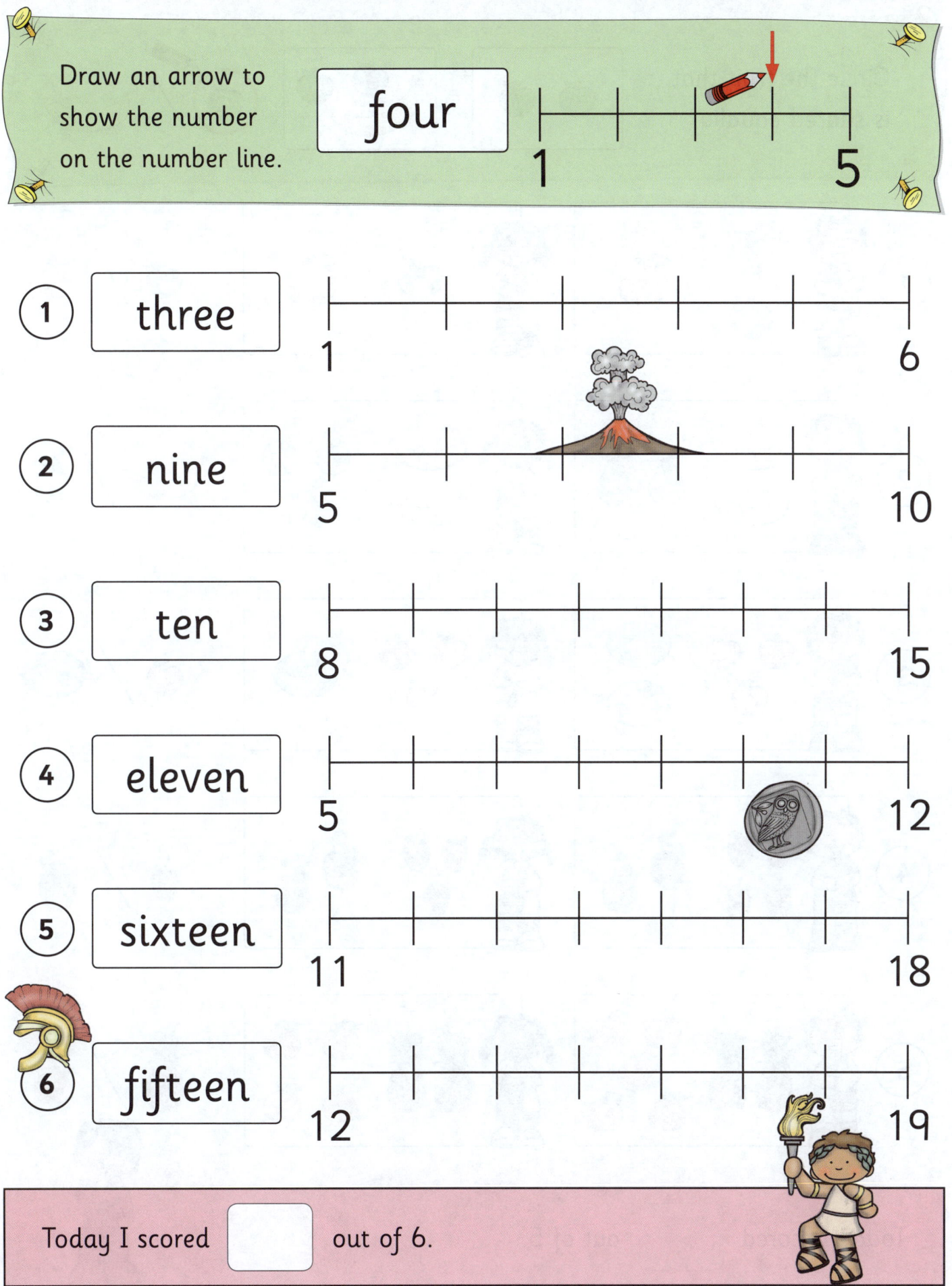

Today I scored ☐ out of 6.

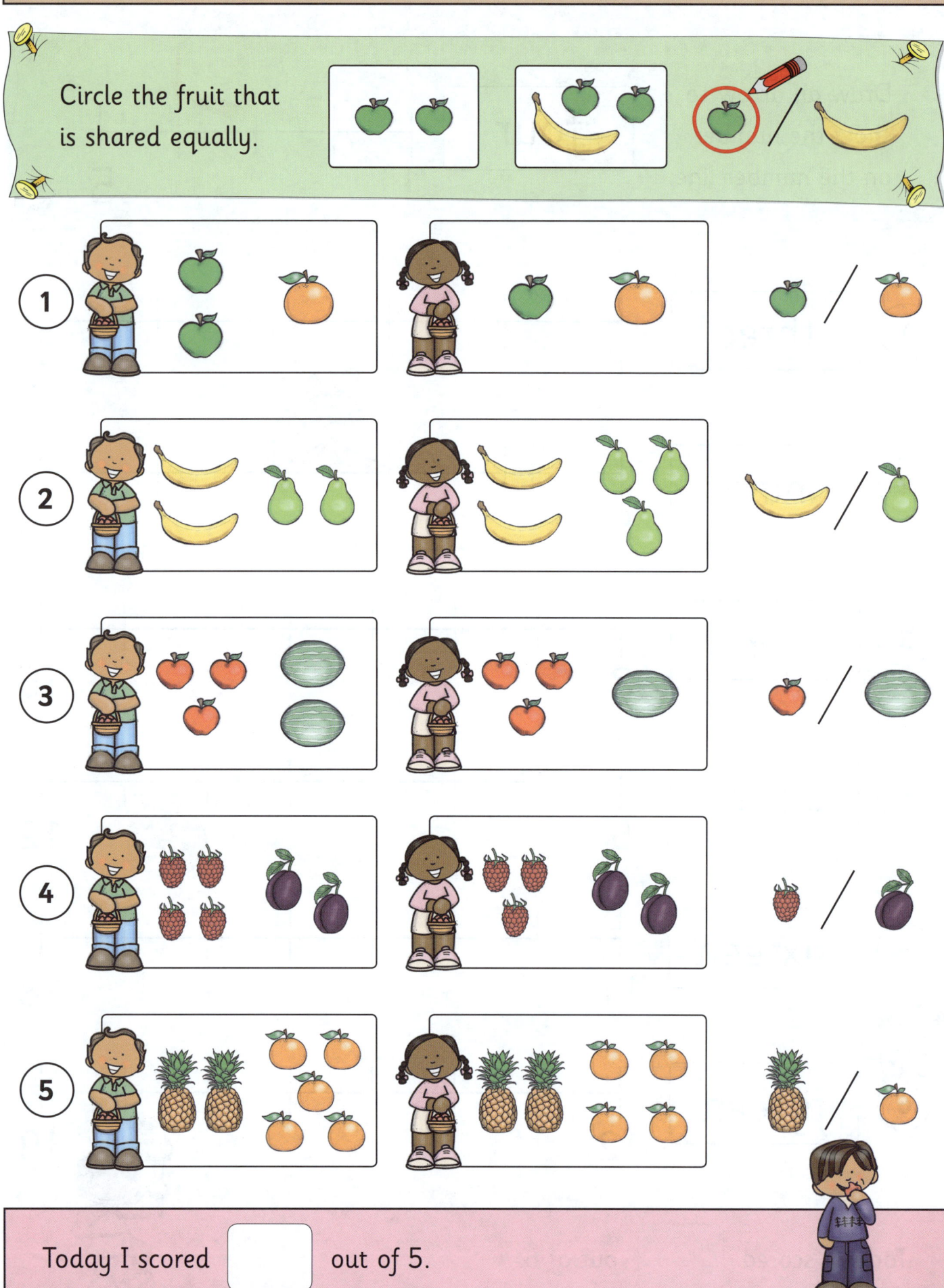

Week 6 — Day 4

Cross out the wrong word.   pig is ~~lighter~~ 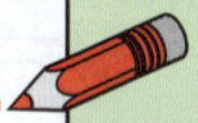 / heavier than string

1. key is lighter / heavier than plane  
2. bag is lighter / heavier than nut  
3. cow is lighter / heavier than scarf  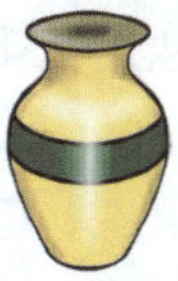
4. ring is lighter / heavier than vase  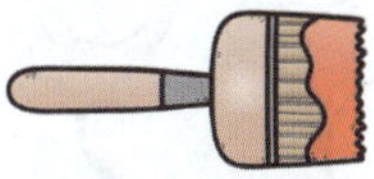
5. bed is lighter / heavier than brush  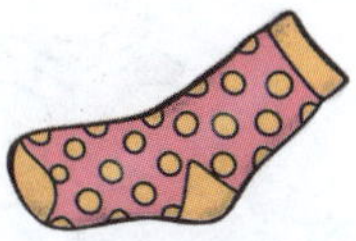
6. pan is lighter / heavier than sock

Today I scored ☐ out of 6.

Week 6 — Day 5

Fill in the answer. 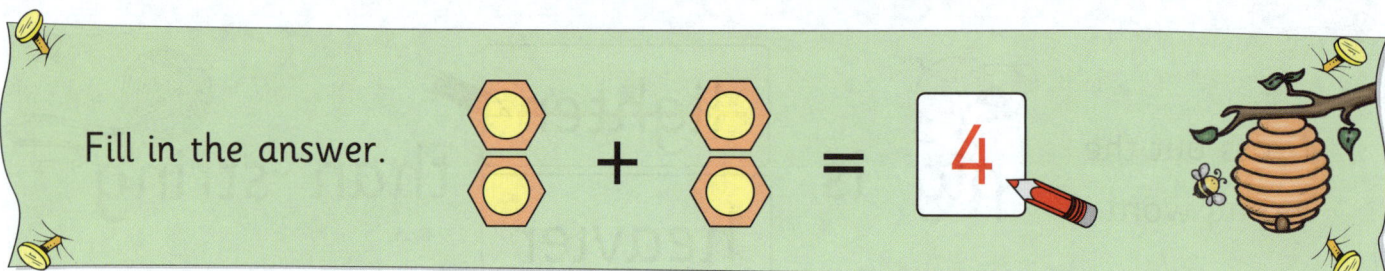 = 4

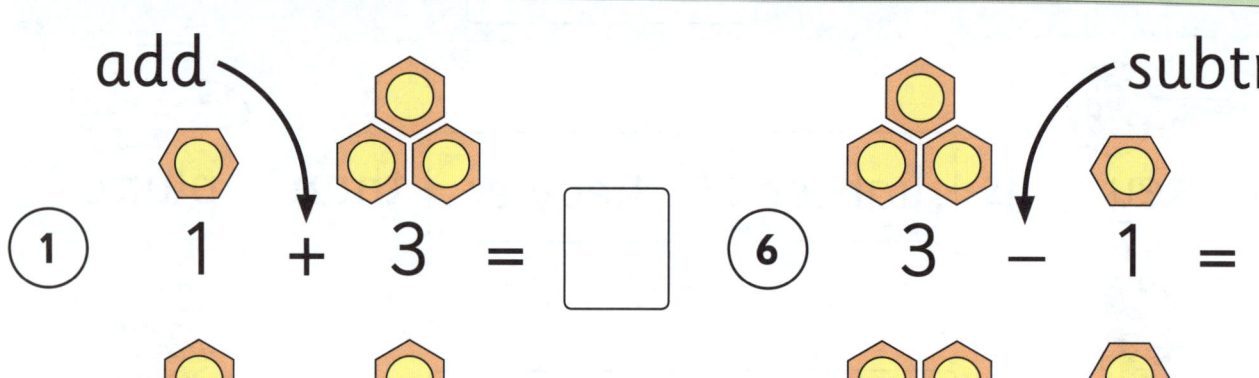

add

1) 1 + 3 = ☐

subtract

6) 3 − 1 = ☐

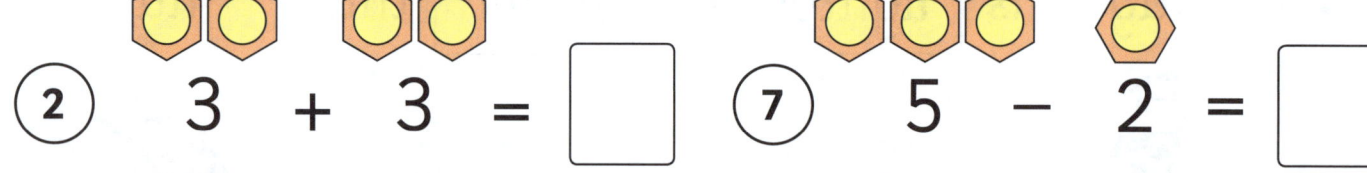

2) 3 + 3 = ☐   7) 5 − 2 = ☐

3) 5 + 2 = ☐   8) 4 − 3 = ☐

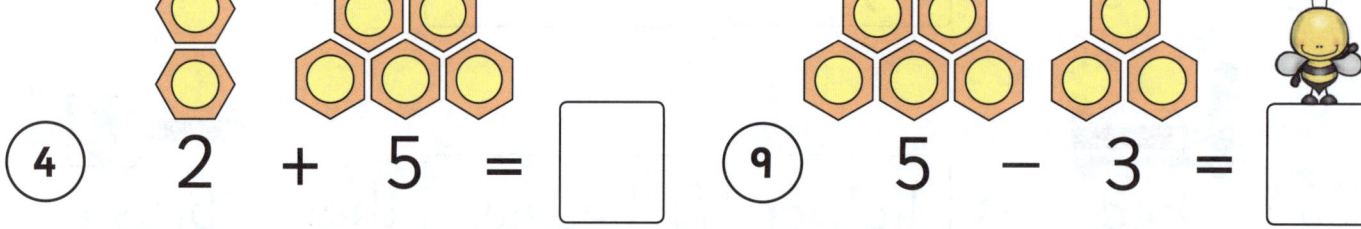

4) 2 + 5 = ☐   9) 5 − 3 = ☐

5) 3 + 4 = ☐   10) 4 − 4 = ☐

Today I scored ☐ out of 10.

Week 7 — Day 1

Cross out the two numbers that you do not say.

Count from 1 to 5.

1. Count from 4 to 8.

2. Count from 6 to 11.

3. Count from 9 to 3.

4. Count from 16 to 12.

5. Count from 19 to 14.

Today I scored ☐ out of 10.

Week 7 — Day 2

Add the numbers. Colour in the number line to help you.

$1 + 2 = 3$

1) $3 + 1 = $

2) $2 + 2 = $

3) $4 + 3 = $

4) $2 + 4 = $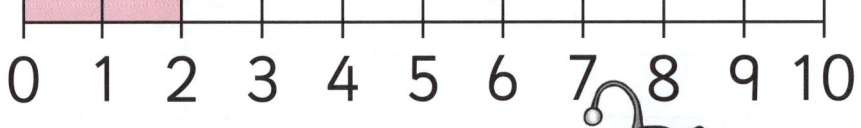

5) $3 + 5 = $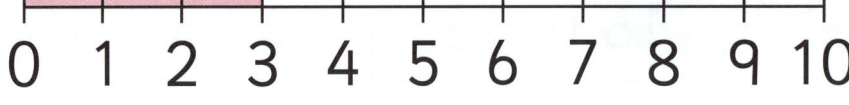

6) $2 + 7 = $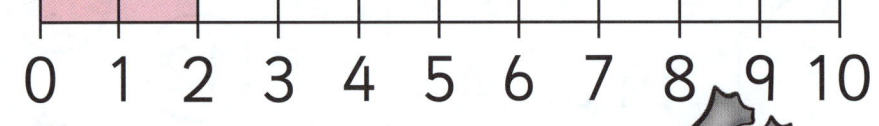

Today I scored ☐ out of 6.

Week 7 — Day 3

Draw lines to match each box to the correct number. Use the pictures to help you.

1.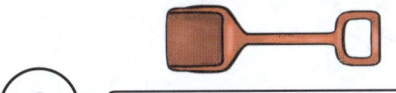
   Double 1

2.
   Double 4

3.
   Double 3

4.
   Double 6

5.
   Double 5

9

10

14

8

12

5

6

2

Today I scored ☐ out of 5.

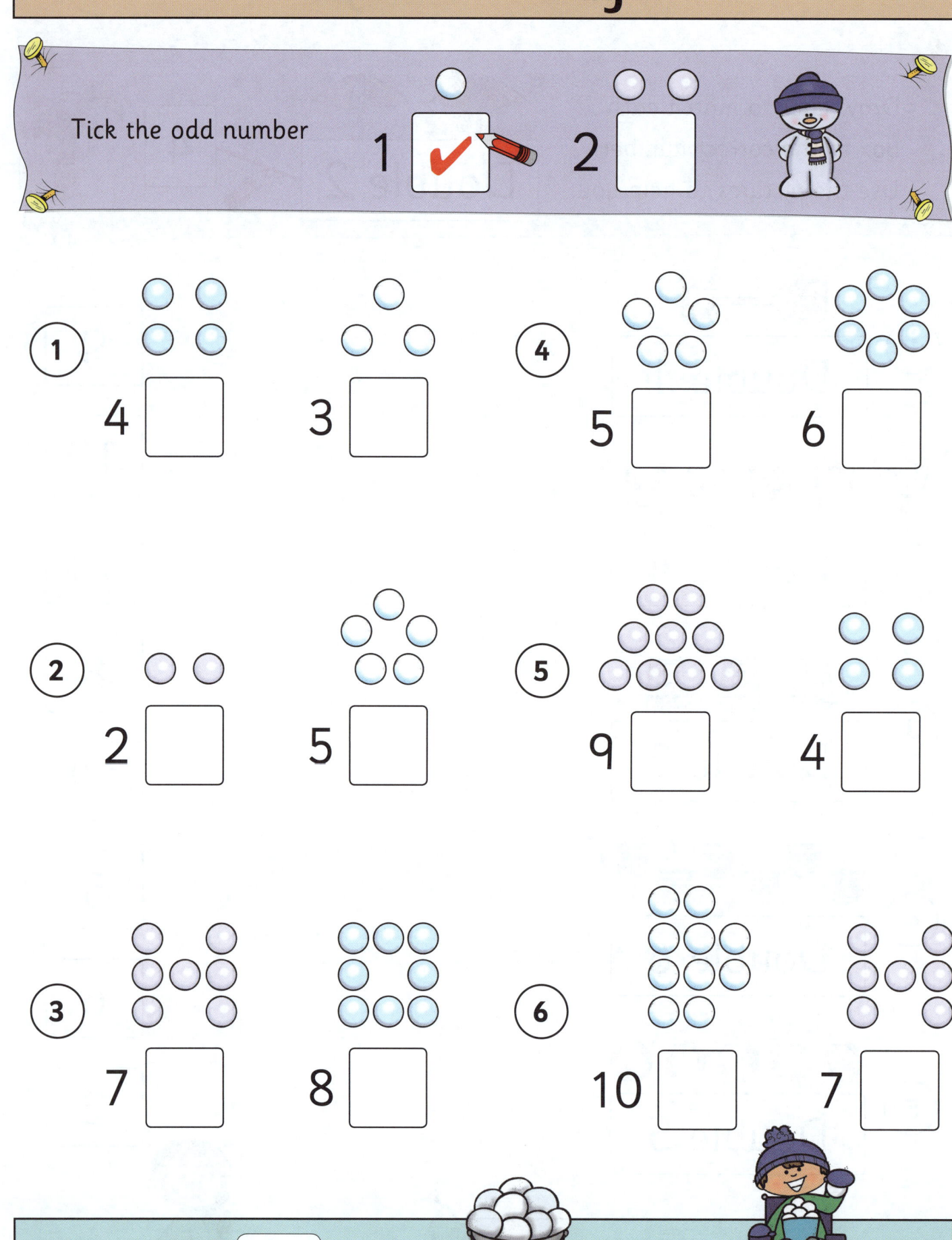

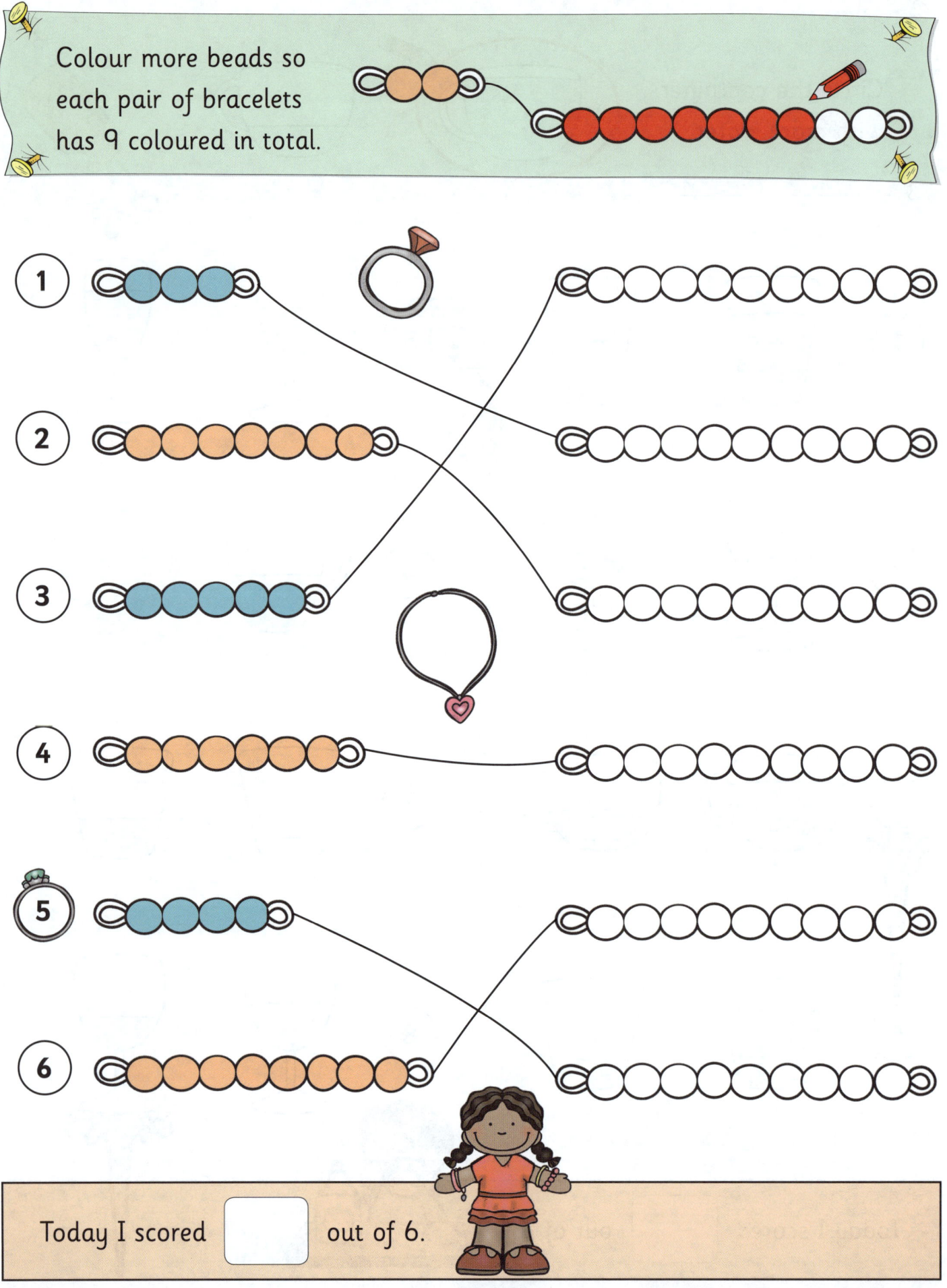

Week 8 — Day 2

Circle two objects that match the word.

cube

① sphere

② cube

③ cylinder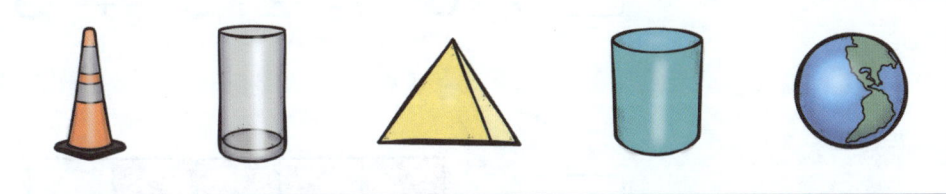

④ cuboid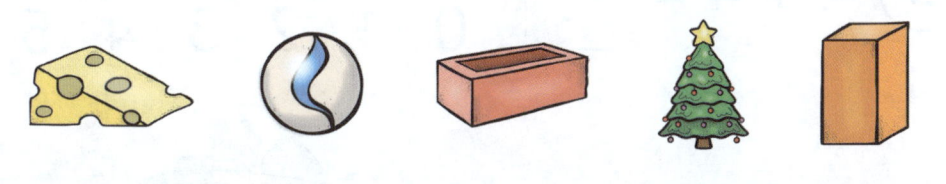

⑤ cone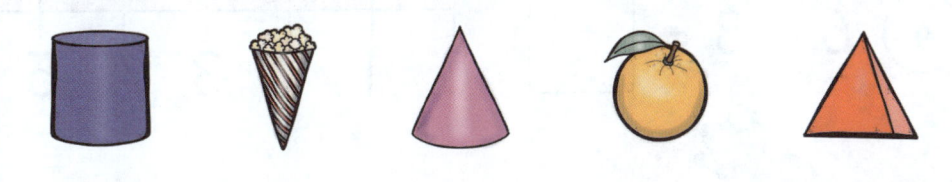

⑥ pyramid

Today I scored ☐ out of 12.

Week 8 — Day 3

Add the numbers. Colour the number line to help you.

3 + 1 = 4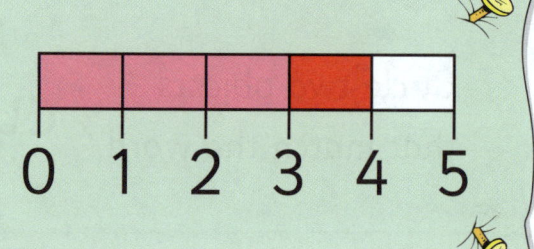

① 6 + 2 = ☐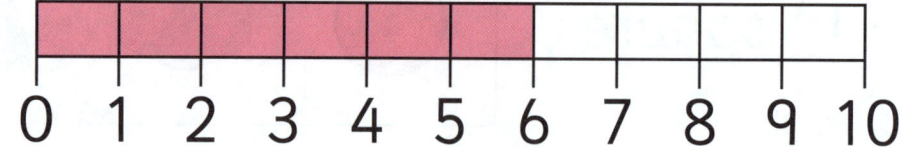

② 3 + 6 = ☐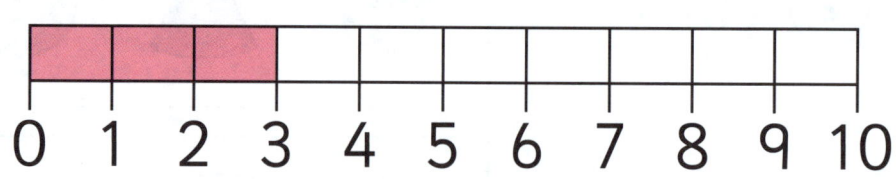

③ 4 + 4 = ☐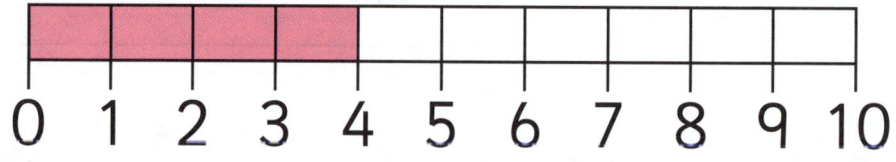

④ 6 + 3 = ☐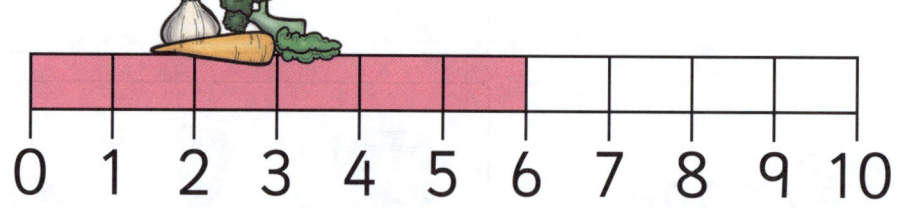

⑤ 5 + 5 = ☐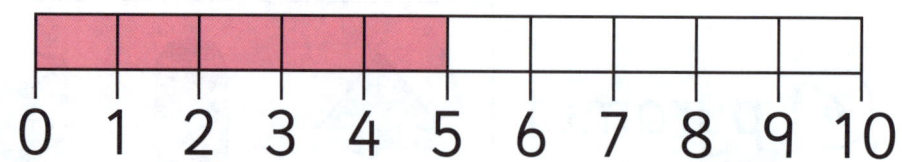

Today I scored ☐ out of 5.

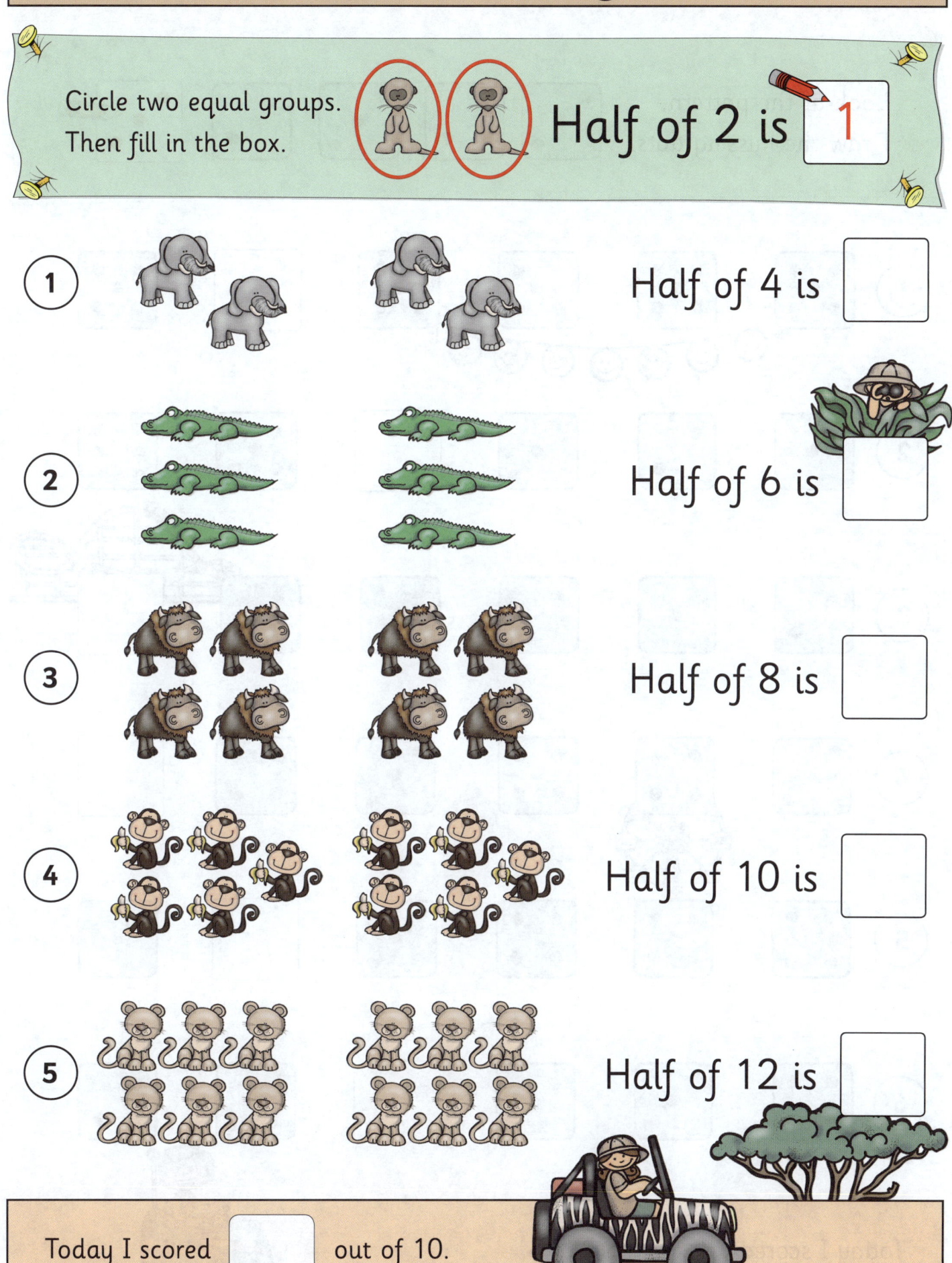

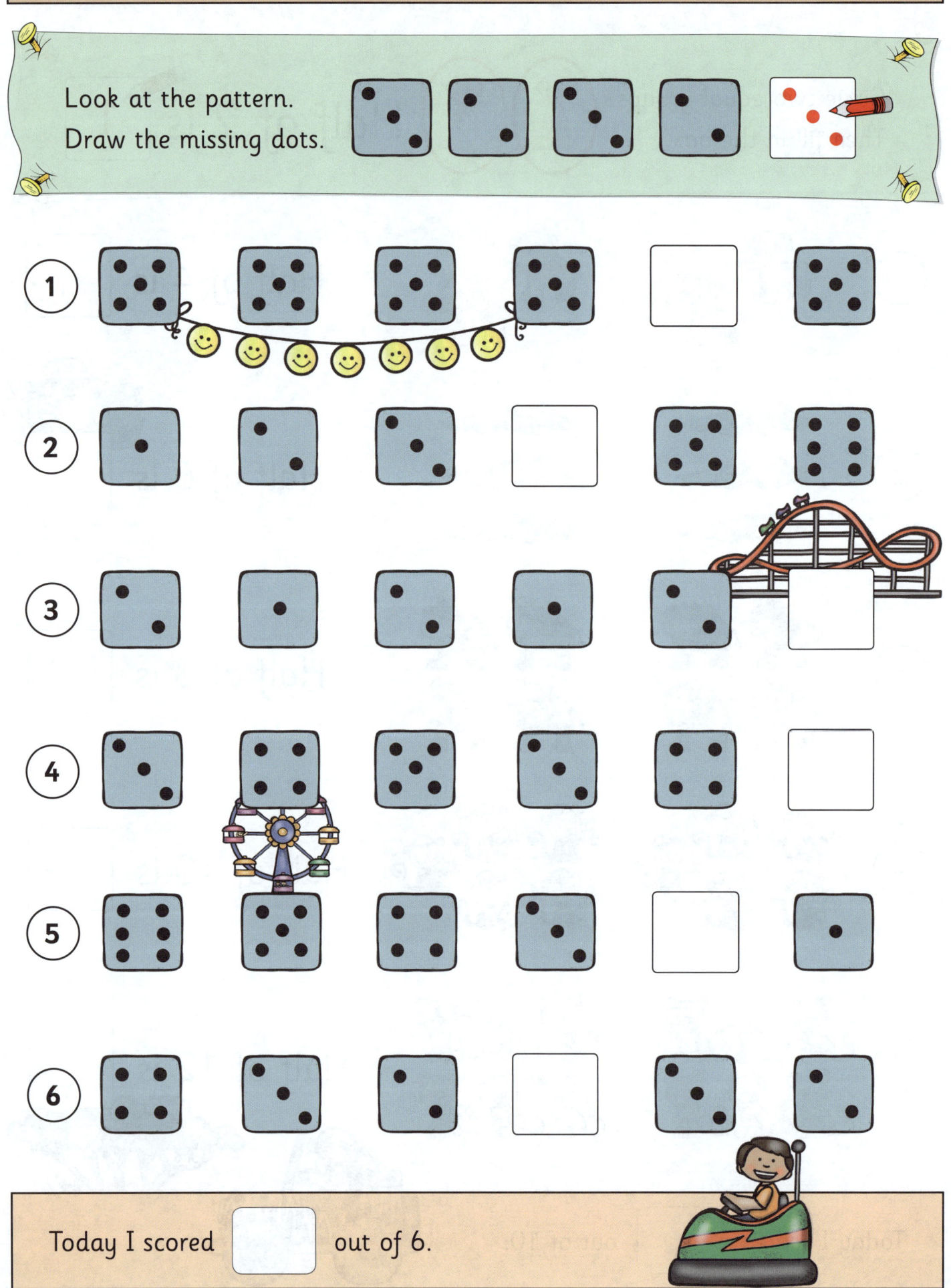

Week 9 — Day 1

Draw a circle in the right place. **Above the square.**

① Below the square.
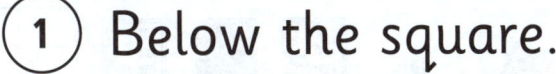

② Left of the triangle.
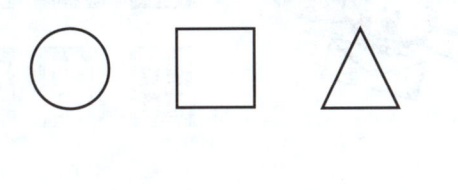

③ Above a rectangle.
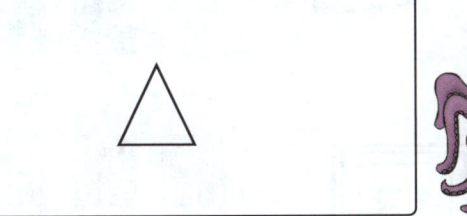

④ Right of the star.

⑤ Next to the square.

⑥ Under a diamond.
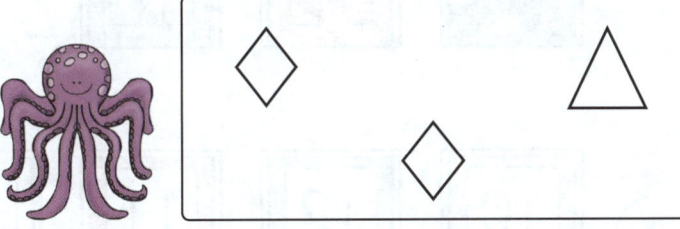

⑦ Between the ovals.
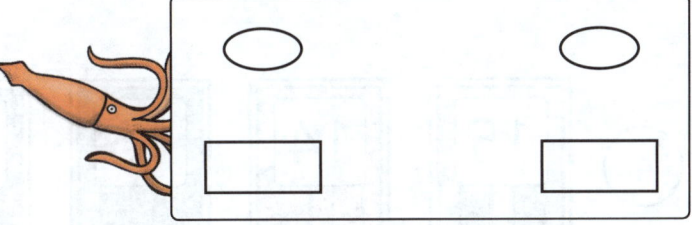

⑧ Inside the triangle.

Today I scored ☐ out of 8.

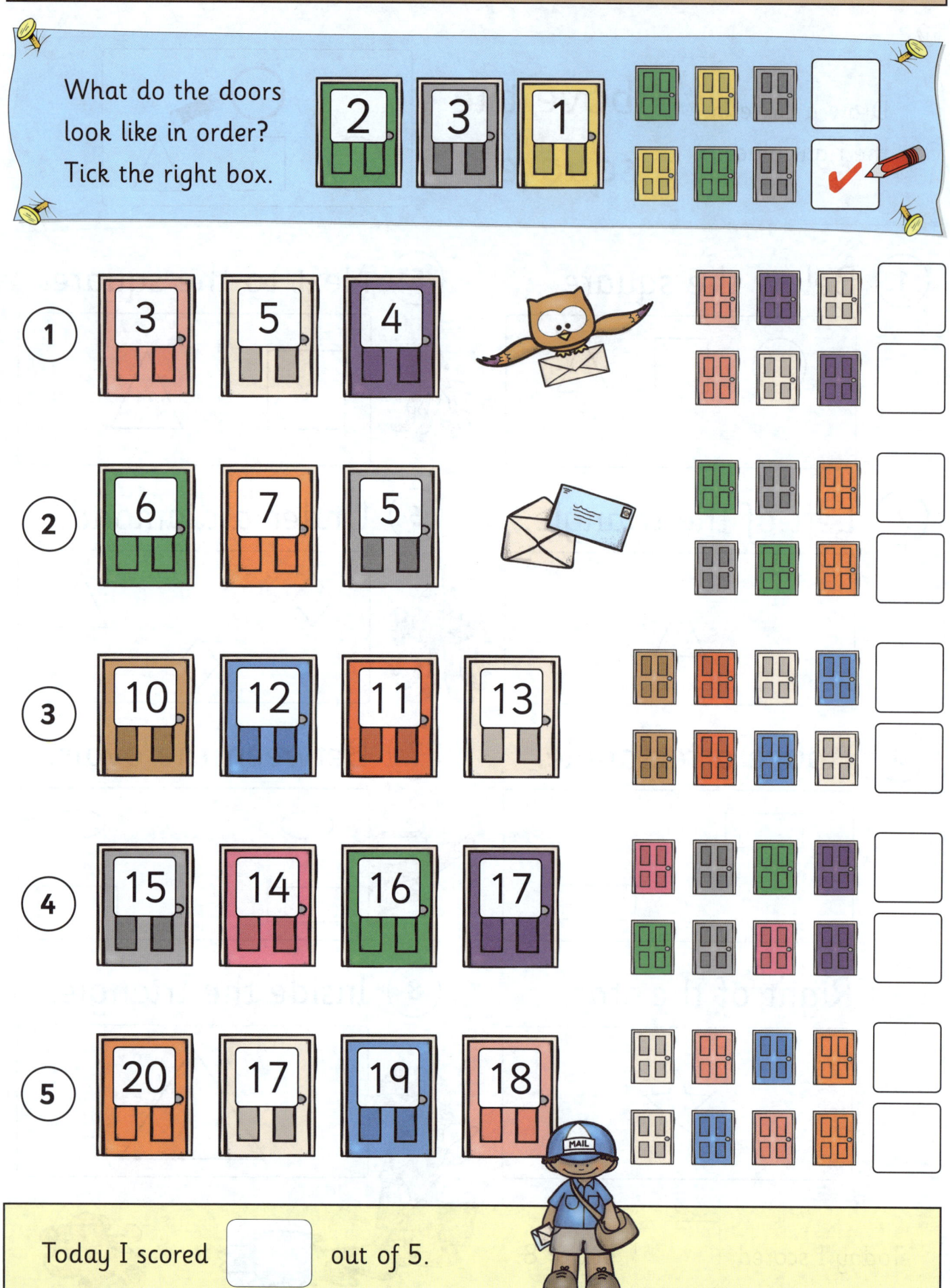

Week 9 — Day 3

Do the subtraction. Circle the answer on the number line.

8 − 2

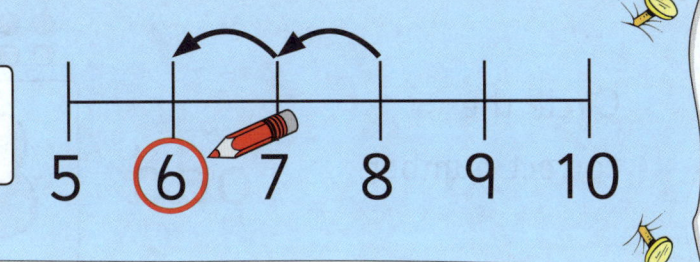

1) 7 − 3

2) 8 − 4

3) 9 − 2

4) 6 − 4

5) 9 − 3

Today I scored ☐ out of 5.

Week 9 — Day 4

Circle the correct number.

odd 8 **5**

1) even 2 3

2) even 5 4

3) even 8 1

4) even 6 5

5) odd 7 8

6) odd 1 2

7) odd 6 9

8) odd 4 3

Today I scored ☐ out of 8.

Reception Maths — Summer Term

Week 9 — Day 5

Share the toys equally. How many toys does each person get?

1   ☐   5   ☐

2   ☐   6  ☐

3     ☐   7     ☐

4   ☐   8    ☐

Today I scored ☐ out of 8.

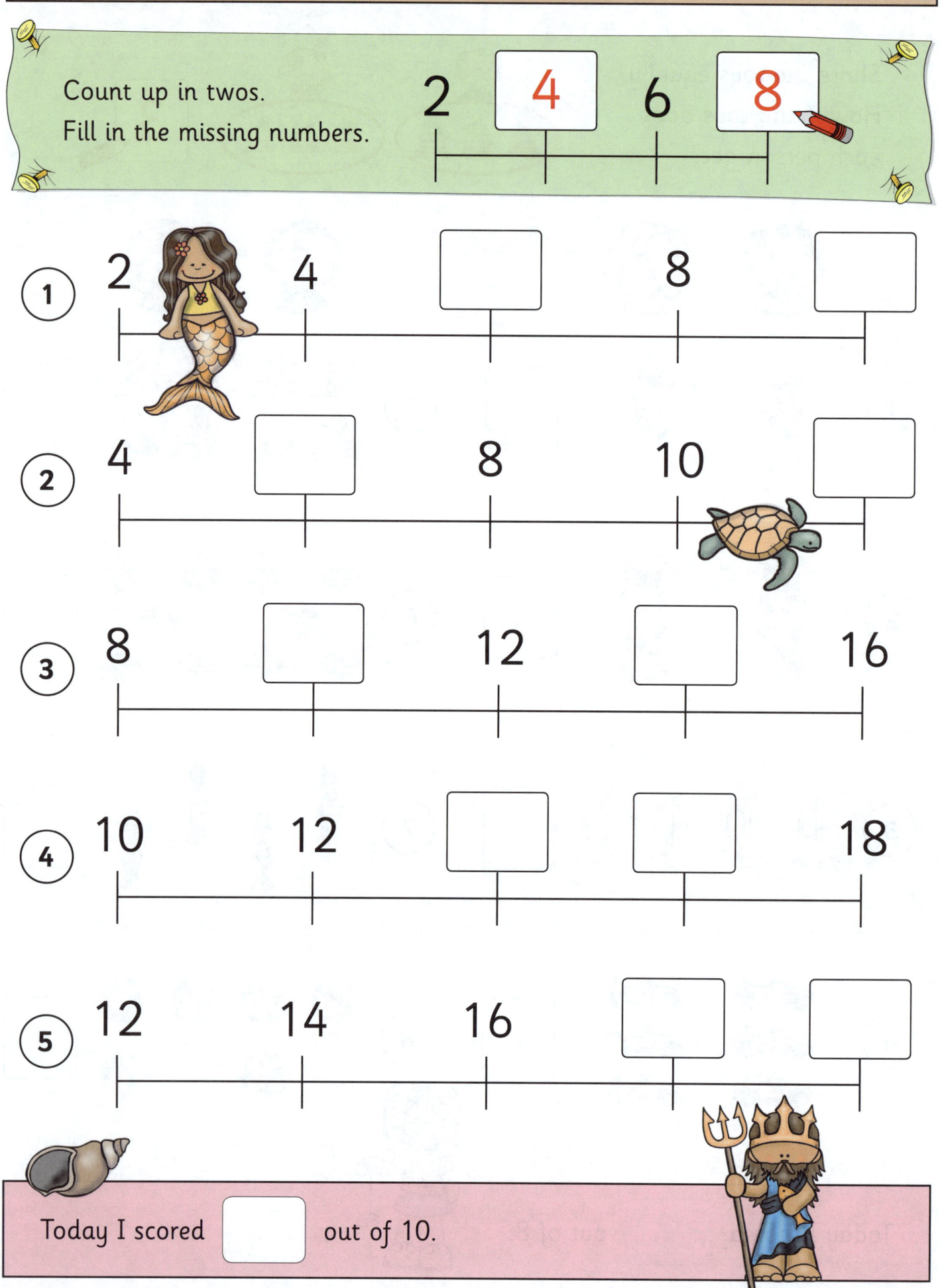

Week 10 — Day 2

Fill in the answer. Use the number line to help you.

4 − 3 = 1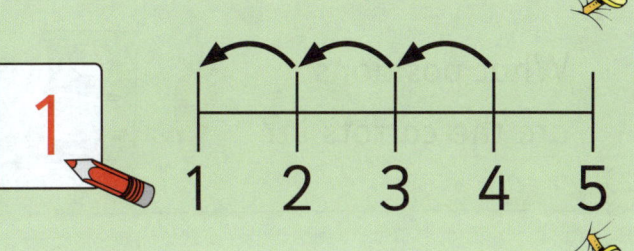

1) 6 − 2 =

2) 7 − 1 =

3) 6 − 5 =

4) 8 − 6 =

5) 9 − 5 =

6) 9 − 7 =

Today I scored ☐ out of 6.

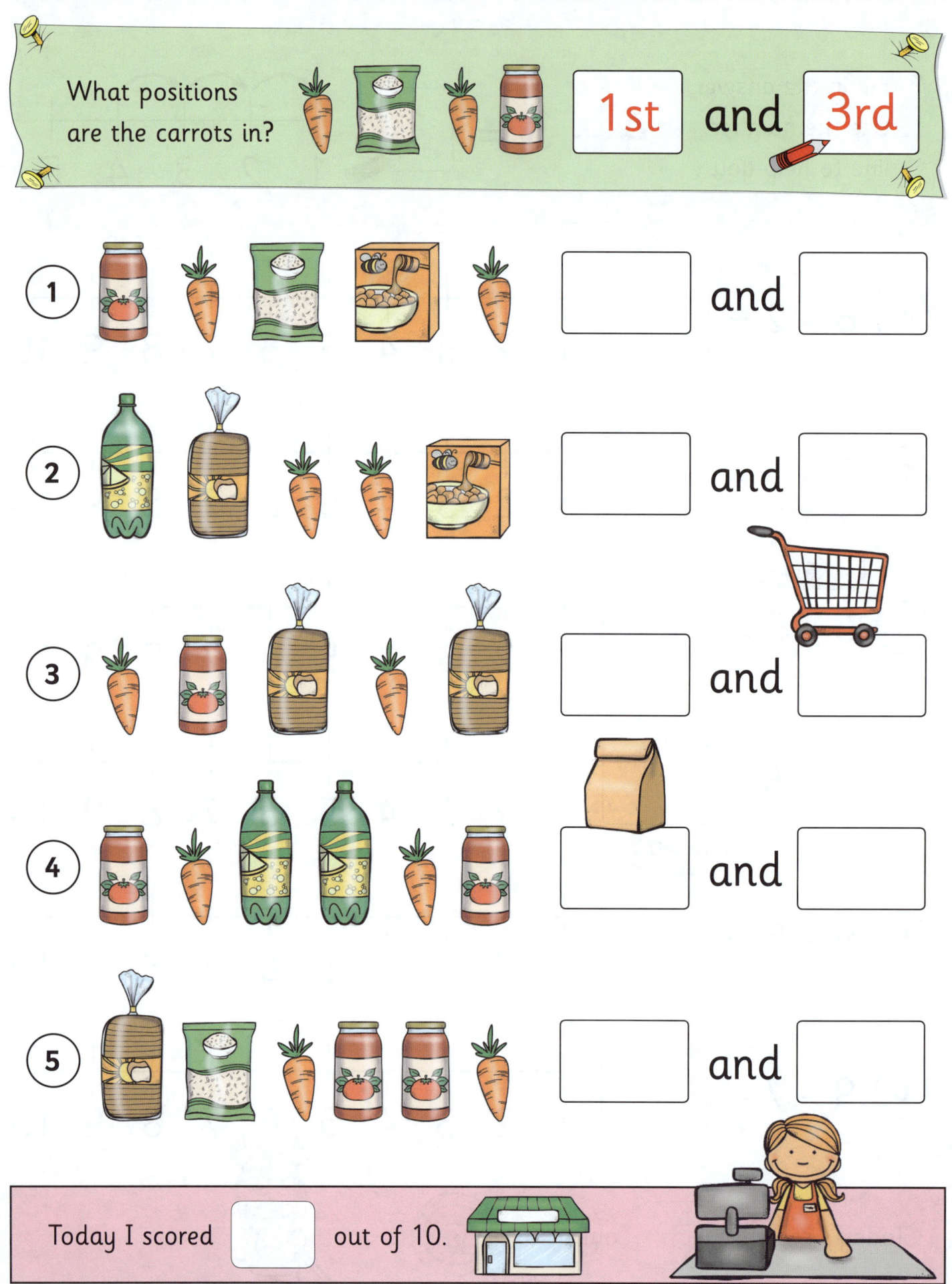

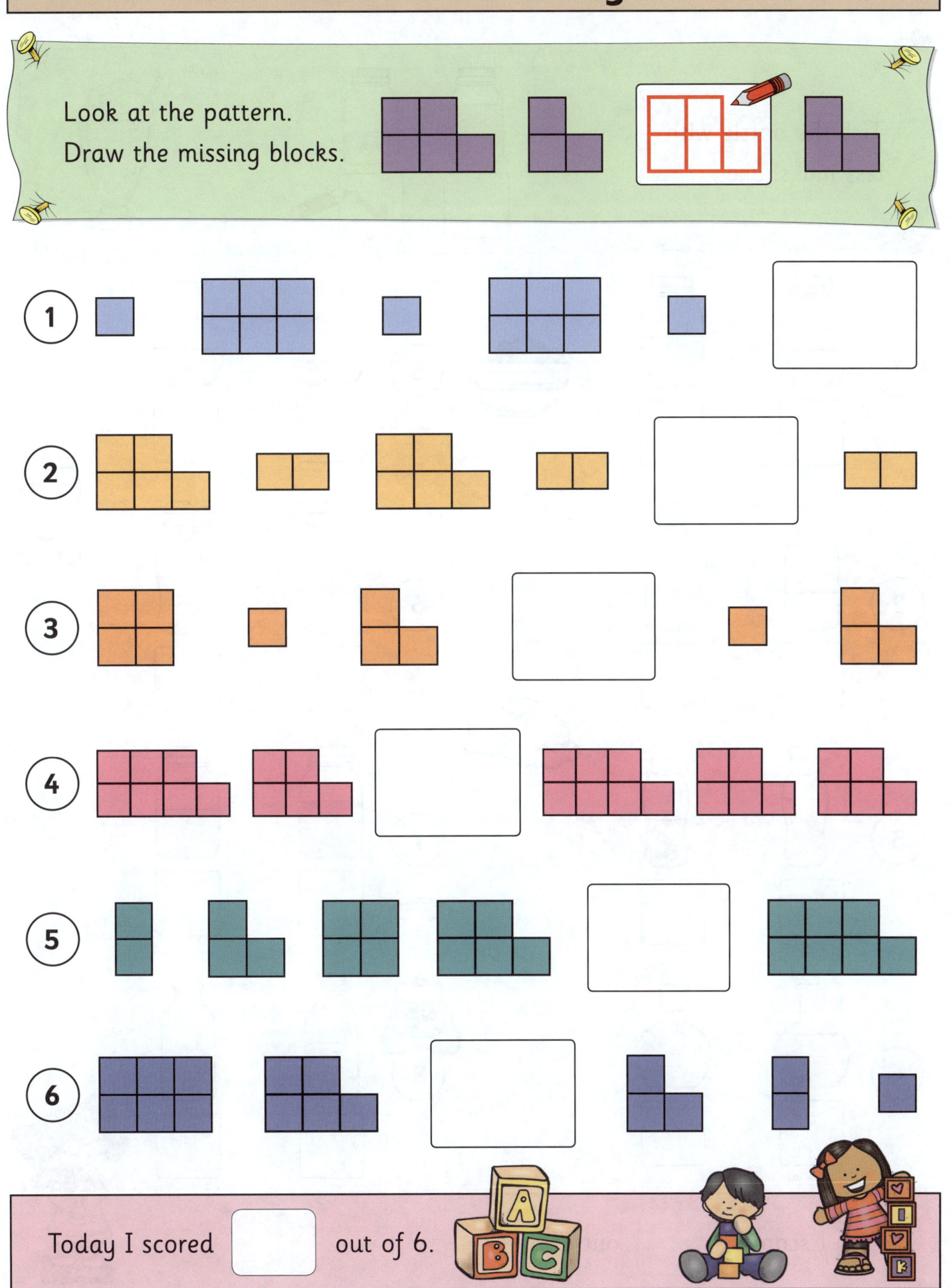

Week 11 — Day 1

Fill in the box to make a sum that adds to 10.

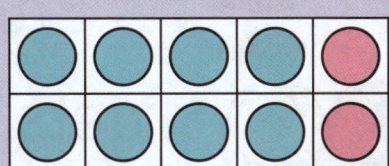 8 + **2**

1. 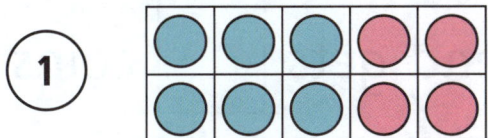 6 + ☐
2. 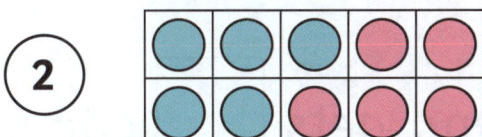 ☐ + 5
3. 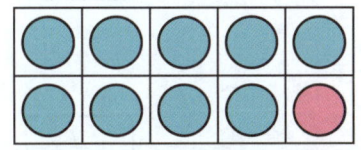 9 + ☐
4. 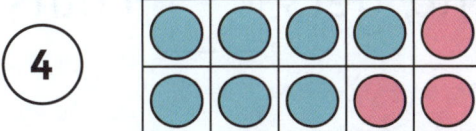 7 + ☐
5. 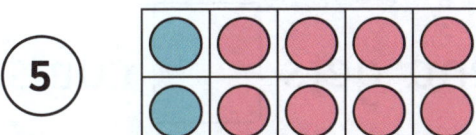 ☐ + 8
6. 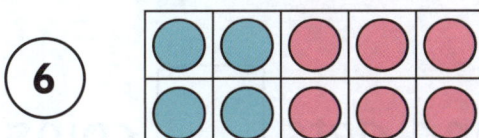 ☐ + 6
7. 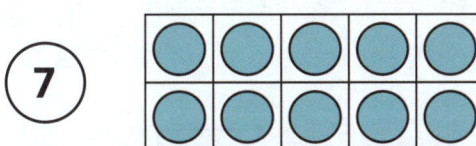 10 + ☐
8. 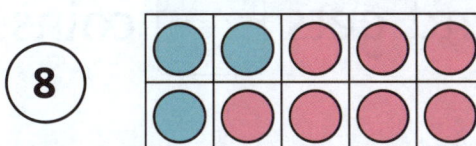 3 + ☐

Today I scored ☐ out of 8.

Week 11 — Day 2

Share the coins equally between two friends. Complete the sentence.

Each friend gets **2** coins.

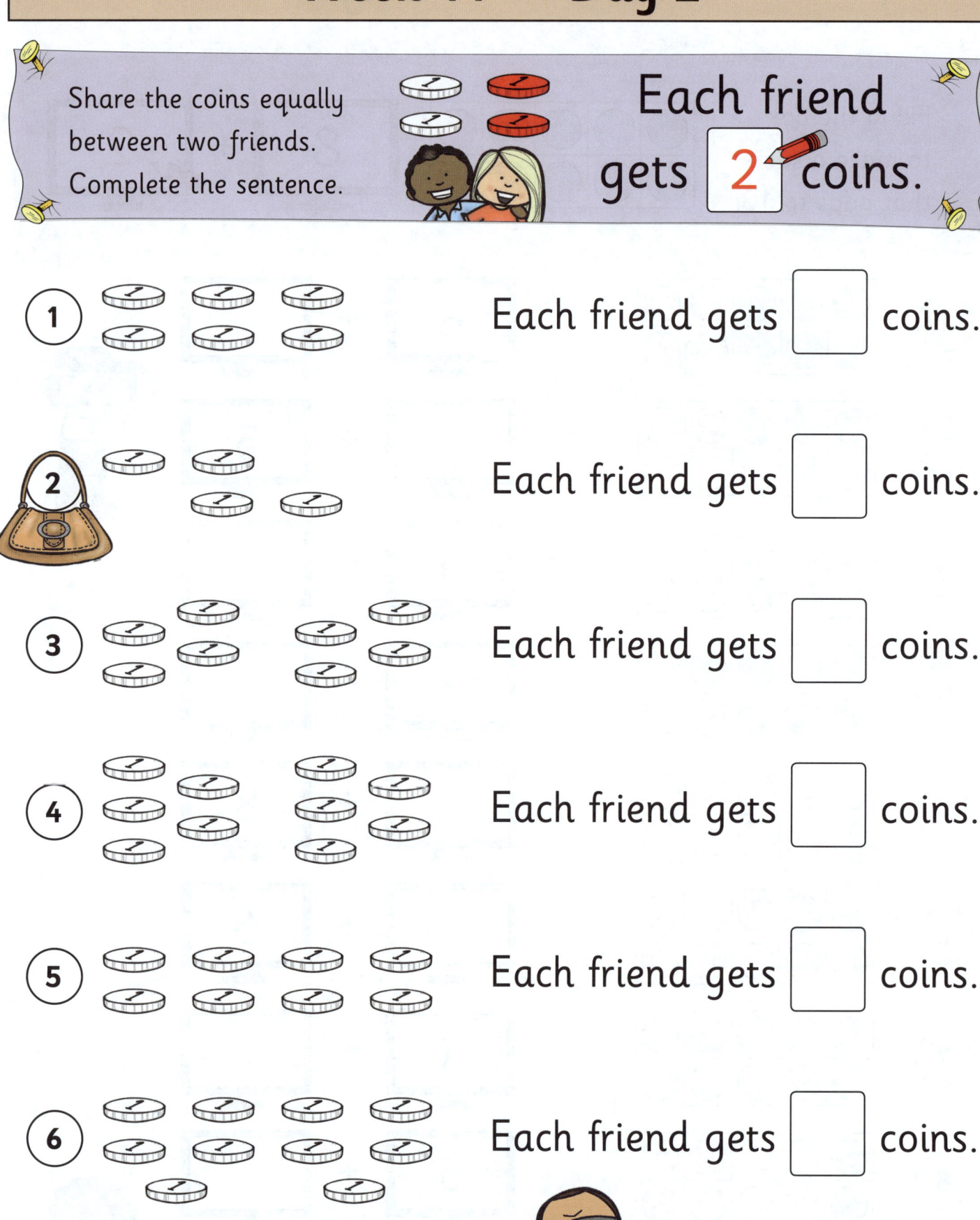

1. Each friend gets ☐ coins.
2. Each friend gets ☐ coins.
3. Each friend gets ☐ coins.
4. Each friend gets ☐ coins.
5. Each friend gets ☐ coins.
6. Each friend gets ☐ coins.

Today I scored ☐ out of 6.

Reception Maths — Summer Term

Week 11 — Day 3

Fill in the answer. Use the number line to help you.

$3 + 2 = 5$

1 2 3 4 5

1 2 3 4 5 6 7 8 9 10

① $4 + 1 = $ ☐   ⑥ $6 - 3 = $ ☐

② $5 + 2 = $ ☐   ⑦ $7 - 6 = $ ☐

③ $3 + 3 = $ ☐   ⑧ $8 - 5 = $ ☐

④ $6 + 3 = $ ☐   ⑨ $10 - 4 = $ ☐

⑤ $2 + 6 = $ ☐   ⑩ $10 - 7 = $ ☐

Today I scored ☐ out of 10.

Week 11 — Day 4

Count forwards to fill in the missing numbers.

| 19 | 20 | **21** |

1) | 11 | 12 | 13 | 14 | |

2) | 17 | | 19 | 20 | 21 |

3) | 12 | 13 | | 15 | |

4) | 20 | 21 | 22 | | 24 |

5) | 18 | | 20 | 21 | |

6) | 23 | 24 | 25 | 26 | |

Today I scored ☐ out of 8.

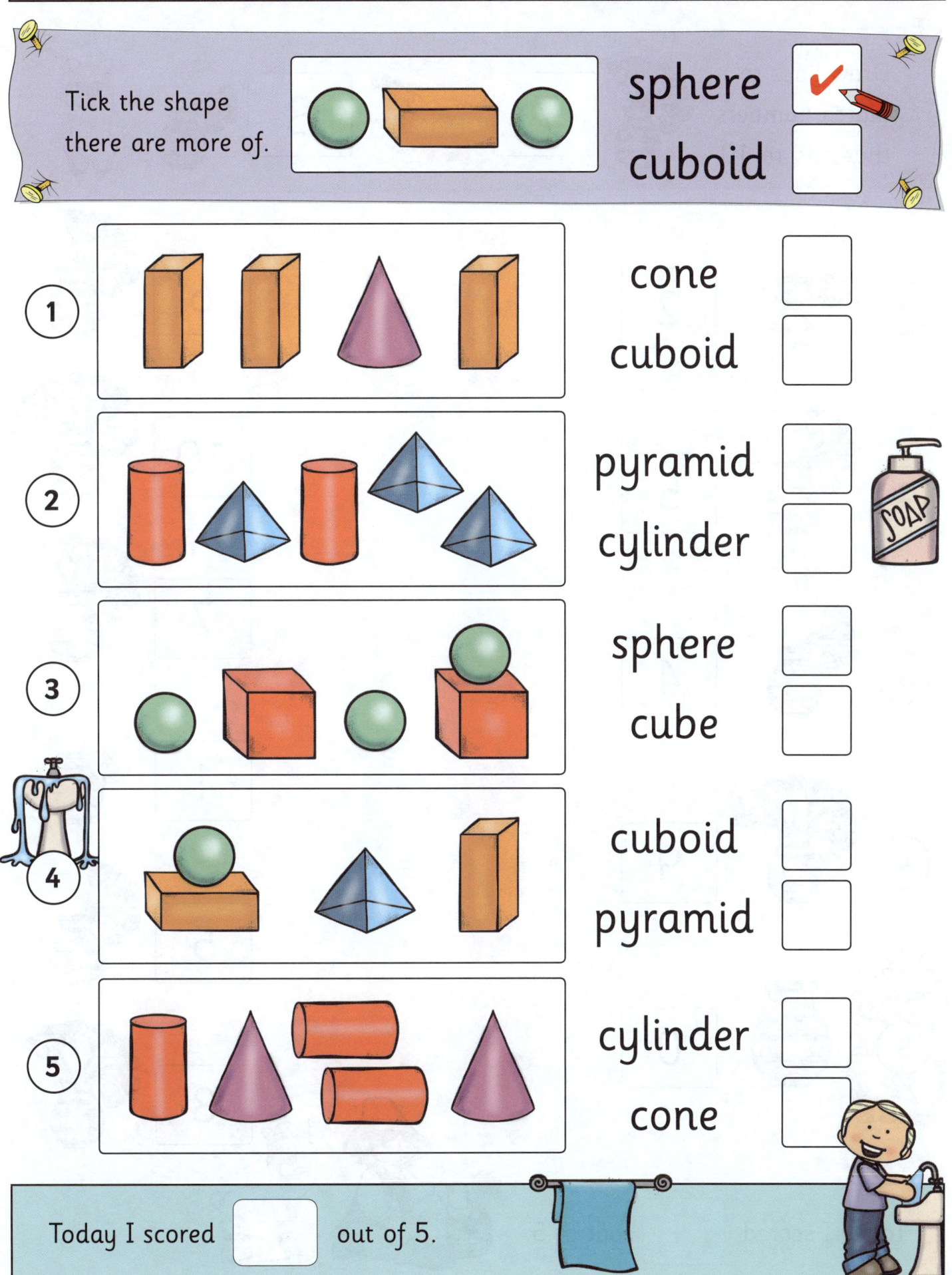

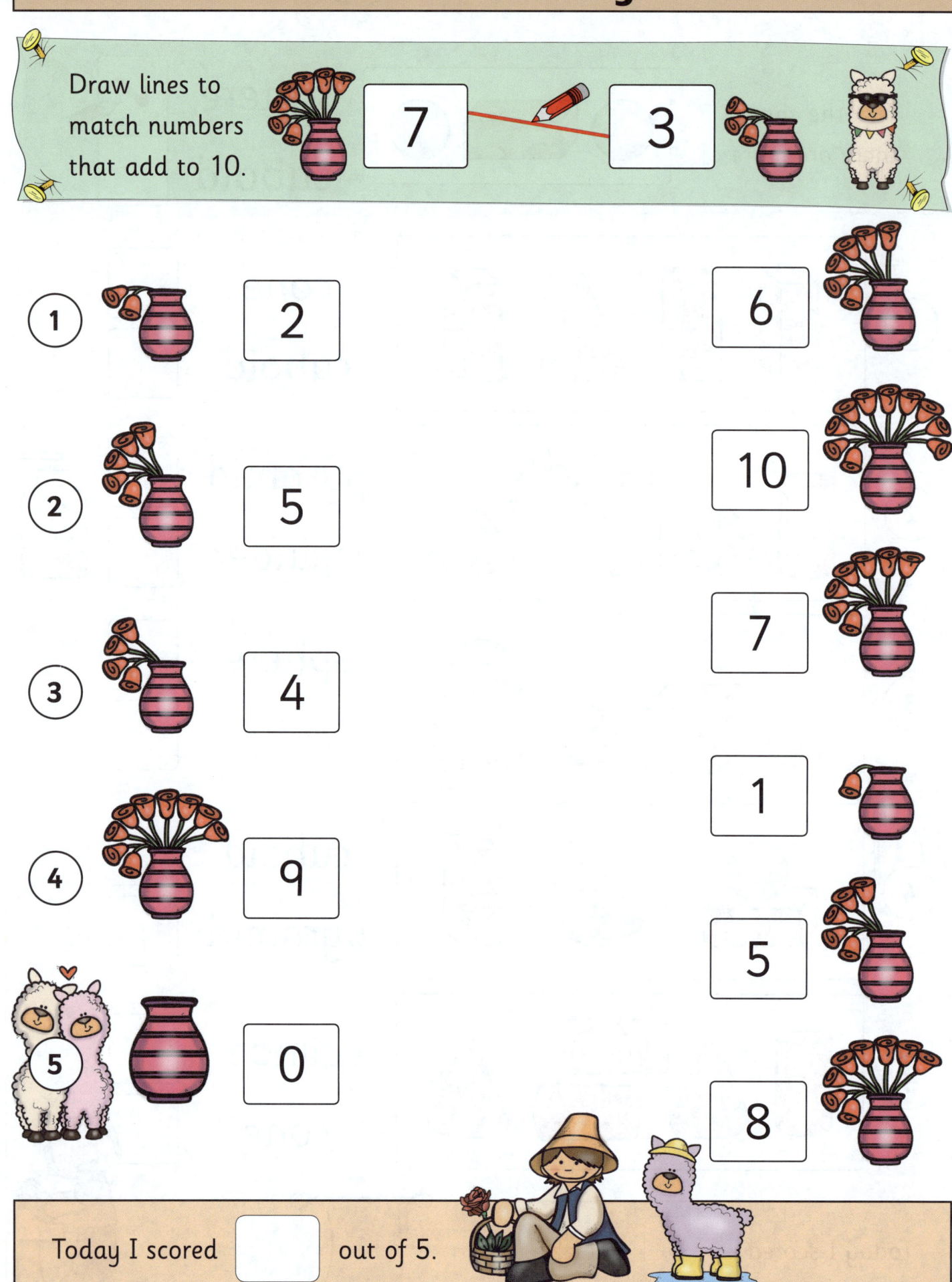

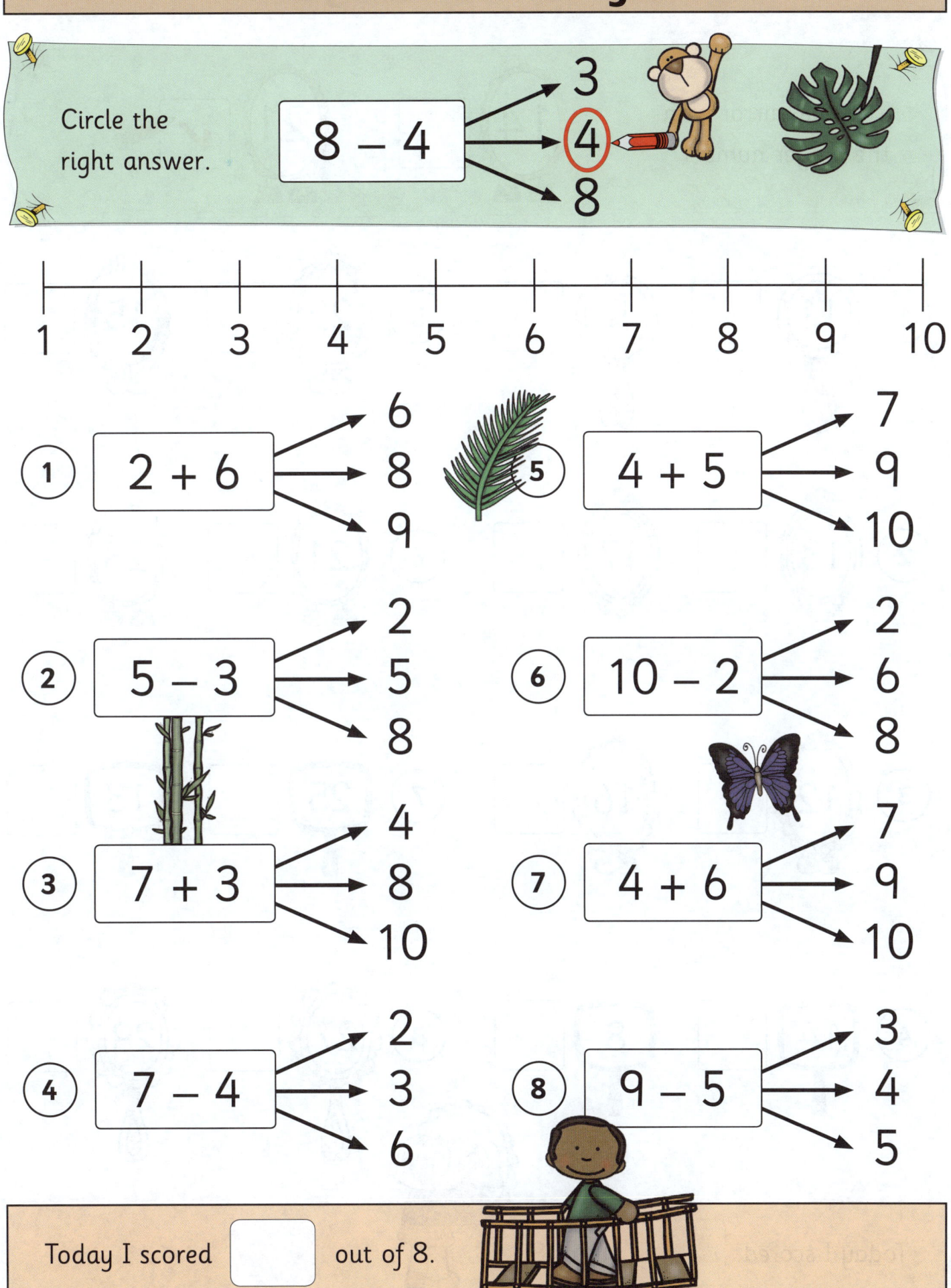

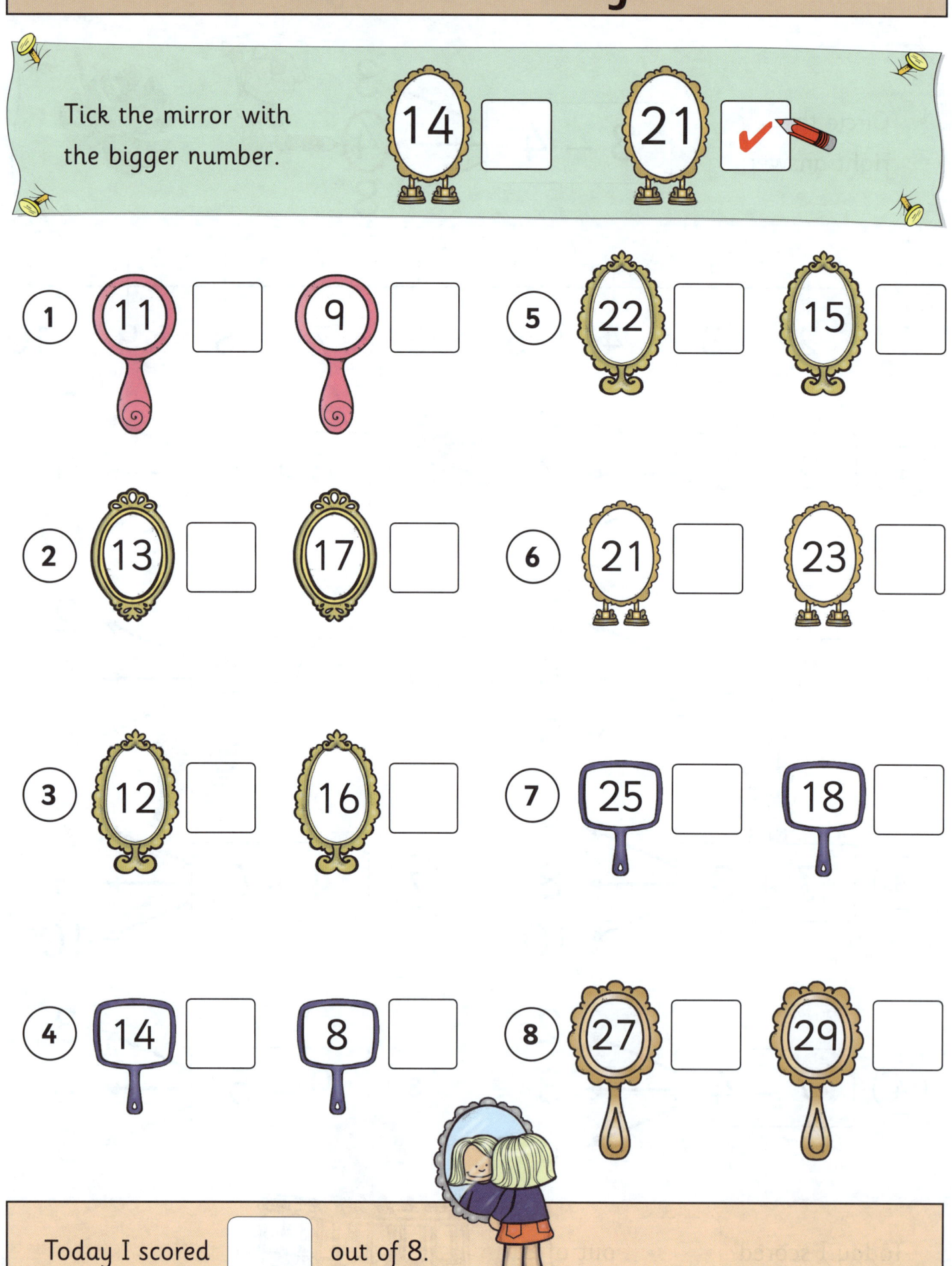

Week 12 — Day 4

Count up in twos.
Circle the wrong number.

2   4   ⑤   8   10

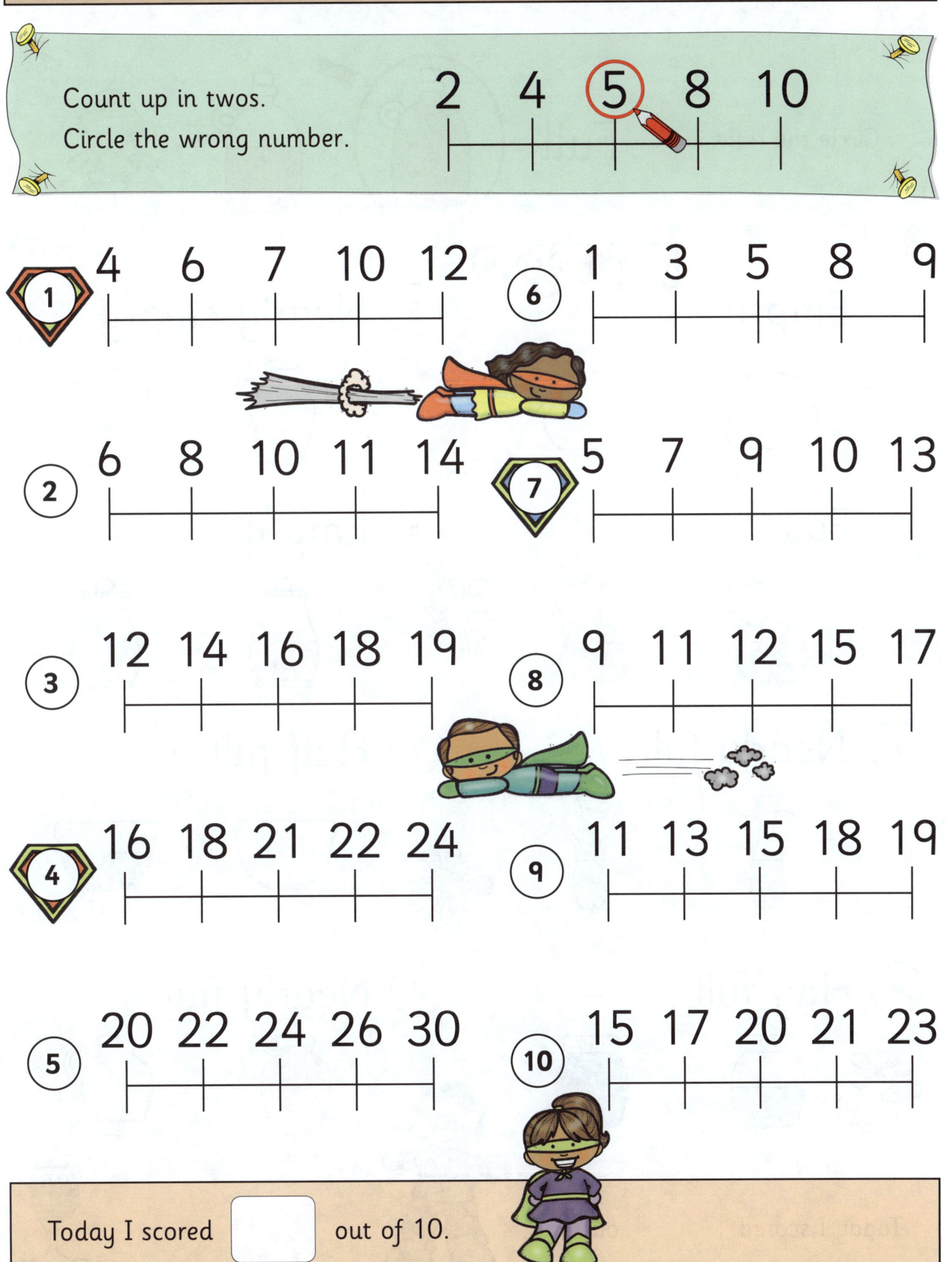

1) 4 6 7 10 12
2) 6 8 10 11 14
3) 12 14 16 18 19
4) 16 18 21 22 24
5) 20 22 24 26 30
6) 1 3 5 8 9
7) 5 7 9 10 13
8) 9 11 12 15 17
9) 11 13 15 18 19
10) 15 17 20 21 23

Today I scored ☐ out of 10.

Week 12 — Day 5

Circle the right jar.   Full

① Empty

② Full

③ Nearly full

④ Half full

⑤ Nearly empty

⑥ Empty

⑦ Half full

⑧ Nearly full

Today I scored ☐ out of 8.

Answers

Week 1 — Day 1

1. / 4.
2. / 5.
3. / 6.

Week 1 — Day 2

Week 1 — Day 3

1. 4 = 2 + **2**
2. 6 = **4** + 2
3. 5 = 3 + **2**
4. 6 = 3 + **3**
5. 7 = **2** + 5
6. 7 = 3 + **4**

Week 1 — Day 4

1. 4 3 2
2. 5 4 3
3. 10 9 8
4. 14 13 12
5. 11 10 9
6. 15 14 13
7. 17 16 15
8. 20 19 18

Week 1 — Day 5

1. 3
2. 3
3. 4
4. 5
5. 5
6. 2
7. 5
8. 5
9. 5
10. 6

Week 2 — Day 1

Week 2 — Day 2

1. solid
2. flat
3. solid
4. flat
5. solid
6. flat
7. solid
8. solid
9. flat
10. flat

Week 2 — Day 3

Week 2 — Day 4

Week 2 — Day 5

1. 1
2. 3
3. 1
4. 2
5. 0
6. 3
7. 1
8. 2

Week 3 — Day 1

1. 0 — **3** — 5
2. 5 — **8** — 10
3. 10 **11** — 15
4. 10 — **13** — 15
5. 15 — **19** 20
6. 15 **17** — 20

Week 3 — Day 2

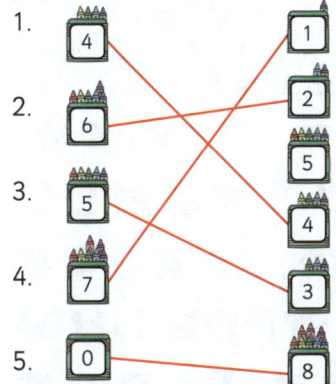

Week 3 — Day 3

Week 3 — Day 4

1. 2
2. 4
3. 1
4. 2
5. 5
6. 1
7. 6
8. 2

Week 3 — Day 5

© CGP — Not to be photocopied  Answers

Week 4 — Day 1
1. 4
2. 6
3. 2
4. 6
5. 7
6. 7
7. 4
8. 6
9. 8
10. 8

Week 4 — Day 2
1. 6
2. 4
3. 10
4. 8
5. 12

Week 4 — Day 3
1. 6
2. 8
3. 4
4. 2
5. 6
6. 10

Week 4 — Day 4
1.
2.
3.
4.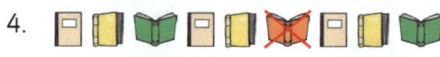
5.
6.
7.

Week 4 — Day 5
1.
2.
3.
4.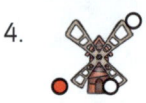
5.
6.
7.
8.

Week 5 — Day 1
1. 1
2. 2
3. 4
4. 6
5. 5
6. 0
7. 8
8. 7

Week 5 — Day 2
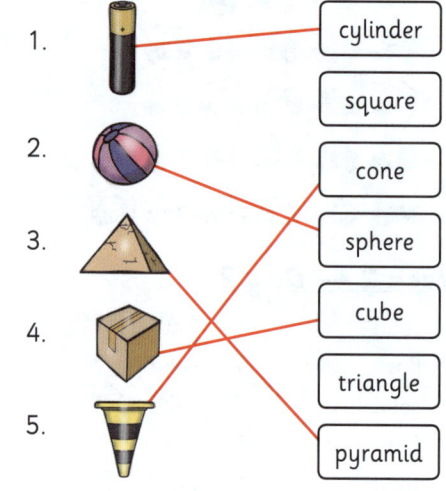

Week 5 — Day 3
1. 2
2. 3
3. 4
4. 5
5. 6

Week 5 — Day 4
1. 7 8 9
2. 9 10 11
3. 11 12 13
4. 12 13 14
5. 15 16 17
6. 13 14 15
7. 18 19 20
8. 17 18 19

Week 5 — Day 5
1. 5
2. 4
3. 6
4. 0
5. 4
6. 2
7. 6
8. 4
9. 1
10. 3

Week 6 — Day 1
1. 2nd
2. 4th
3. 1st
4. 3rd
5. 5th
6. 2nd

Week 6 — Day 2

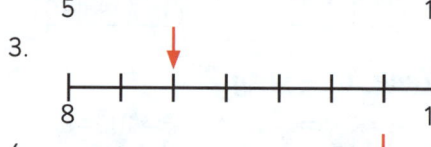
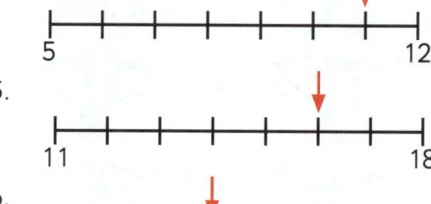
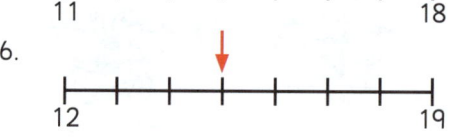

Week 6 — Day 3
1. orange (circled)
2. banana (circled)
3. orange (circled)
4. plum (circled)
5. pineapple (circled)

Week 6 — Day 4
1. lighter / heavier
2. lighter / heavier
3. lighter / heavier
4. lighter / heavier
5. lighter / heavier
6. lighter / heavier

Week 6 — Day 5
1. 4
2. 6
3. 7
4. 7
5. 7
6. 2
7. 3
8. 1
9. 2
10. 0

Week 7 — Day 1
1. 3 and 9
2. 5 and 12
3. 10 and 11
4. 11 and 17
5. 12 and 13

Week 7 — Day 2
1. 4
2. 4
3. 7
4. 6
5. 8
6. 9

Week 7 — Day 3

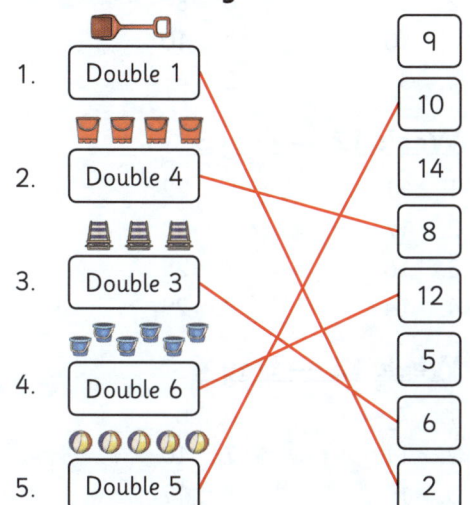

Week 7 — Day 4
1. 3
2. 5
3. 7
4. 5
5. 9
6. 7

Week 7 — Day 5
1.
2.
3.
4.
5.
6.
7.
8.

Week 8 — Day 1
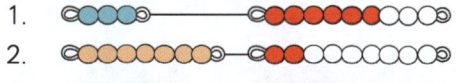

Week 8 — Day 2

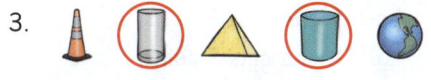

Week 8 — Day 3
1. 8
2. 9
3. 8
4. 9
5. 10

Week 8 — Day 4
1.  Half of 4 is **2**
2.  Half of 6 is **3**
3.  Half of 8 is **4**
4.  Half of 10 is **5**
5.  Half of 12 is **6**

Week 8 — Day 5

Week 9 — Day 1
1.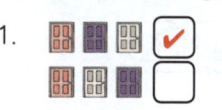
2.
3.
4.
5.
6.
7.
8.

Week 9 — Day 2
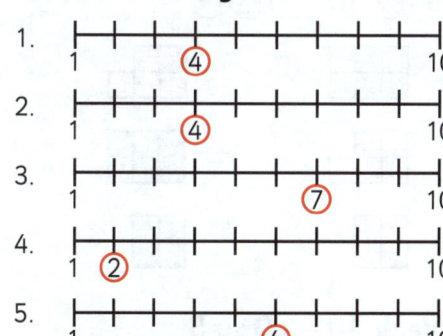

Week 9 — Day 3
1. ④ at 4
2. ④ at 4
3. ⑦ at 7
4. ② at 2
5. ⑥ at 6

Week 9 — Day 4
1. 2
2. 4
3. 8
4. 6
5. 7
6. 1
7. 9
8. 3

Week 9 — Day 5
1. 1
2. 2
3. 2
4. 3
5. 4
6. 5
7. 2
8. 3

64

Week 10 — Day 1
1. 2 4 **6** 8 **10**
2. 4 **6** 8 10 **12**
3. 8 **10** 12 **14** 16
4. 10 12 **14** **16** 18
5. 12 14 16 **18** **20**

Week 10 — Day 2
1. 4
2. 6
3. 1
4. 2
5. 4
6. 2

Week 10 — Day 3
1. **2nd** and **5th**
2. **3rd** and **4th**
3. **1st** and **4th**
4. **2nd** and **5th**
5. **3rd** and **6th**

Week 10 — Day 4

Week 10 — Day 5

Week 11 — Day 1
1. 4
2. 5
3. 1
4. 3
5. 2
6. 4
7. 0
8. 7

Week 11 — Day 2
1. Each friend gets **3** coins.
2. Each friend gets **2** coins.
3. Each friend gets **4** coins.
4. Each friend gets **5** coins.
5. Each friend gets **4** coins.
6. Each friend gets **5** coins.

Week 11 — Day 3
1. 5
2. 7
3. 6
4. 9
5. 8
6. 3
7. 1
8. 3
9. 6
10. 3

Week 11 — Day 4
1. 11 12 13 14 **15**
2. 17 **18** 19 20 21
3. 12 13 **14** 15 **16**
4. 20 21 22 **23** 24
5. 18 **19** 20 21 **22**
6. 23 24 25 26 **27**

Week 11 — Day 5
1. cuboid
2. pyramid
3. sphere
4. cuboid
5. cylinder

Week 12 — Day 1

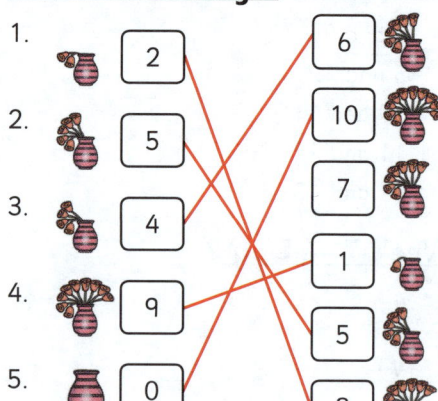

Week 12 — Day 2
1. 8
2. 2
3. 10
4. 3
5. 9
6. 8
7. 10
8. 4

Week 12 — Day 3
1. 11
2. 17
3. 16
4. 14
5. 22
6. 23
7. 25
8. 29

Week 12 — Day 4
1. 7
2. 11
3. 19
4. 21
5. 30
6. 8
7. 10
8. 12
9. 18
10. 20

Week 12 — Day 5

Answers